Reclaiming the Political Process

Reclaiming the Political Process

An Invitation to American Christians
to Get Back in the Fight

RAY MILLER

Foreword by Bill Redmond

WIPF *&* STOCK · Eugene, Oregon

RECLAIMING THE POLITICAL PROCESS
An Invitation to American Christians to Get Back in the Fight

Wipf & Stock
An Imprint of Wipf and Stock Publishers
199 W. 8th Ave., Suite 3
Eugene, OR 97401

www.wipfandstock.com

PAPERBACK ISBN: 979-8-3852-2062-5
HARDCOVER ISBN: 979-8-3852-2063-2
EBOOK ISBN: 979-8-3852-2064-9

04/08/24

In honor of my dear friends, Judge Keith Norwood and Marcella Melendez. Their lives embody the truths I have sought to put into words in this book.

Contents

Foreword

Dear Pastors and Brothers and Sisters in Christ,

This is the book I've been waiting for! Please, join me in thanking Pastor Ray Miller for his shepherd's heart, eagle's vision, and the passionate encouragement that he demonstrates in this little book that carries a powerful punch, *Reclaiming the Political Process: An Invitation to American Christians to Get Back in the Fight*. This book is a much-needed contribution to pastors and ordinary Christians in this current era of crisis for both the church and American society. While many church leaders wring their hands with little to no understanding of current events—let alone knowing what to do—Pastor Ray Miller has taken the time to sort things out and provide both light and direction to many confused Christians, especially pastors.

Speaking as a pastor to other pastors, I say, brother shepherds, we are without excuse! Pastors who have gone before us had warned us of the challenges we face today. That compliant pastor, Martin Niemöller, who was also the son of a pastor, warned us both by word and by deed. He said,

> First they came for the socialists, and I did not speak out—because I was not a socialist. Then they came for the trade unionists, and I did not speak out—because I was not a trade unionist. Then they came for the Jews, and I did not speak out—because I was not a Jew. Then they came for me—and there was no one left to speak for me.[1]

1. "Martin Niemöller."

These words are an indictment on shepherds who do not understand when understanding is available, who are silent when a prophetic word of rebuke and instruction is urgently needed, as well as those who are passive while opportunities for action are plentiful. Pastor Niemöller's words of warning are prominently featured on a wall at the Holocaust Museum in Washington, DC, as the final words of the exhibition, words that are ignored by Christians today, much to our own peril. Let's get back in the fight.

Though Niemöller stood in the pulpit Sunday after Sunday reading from the Gospels, he was antisemitic and supported Hitler in two elections *from the pulpit*! His support was not because he feared Hitler, as many German pastors of that time did, but Niemöller was enthralled with Hitler. How can this be? How can a Christian shepherd be so blind to the evil in his presence and endorse it? Was it perhaps that his liberal theology was only a Kantian and Hegelian idolatry of the human being expressed with a veneer of Judeo-Christian vocabulary? Pastor Niemöller apparently forgot that fiery preacher Paul who warned Christians in the ancient city of Colossae not to be taken captive through the empty and deceptive philosophies of men. Pastor Niemöller was in fact taken captive first by Hitler's philosophy and second by his Gestapo. He was imprisoned for eight years, along with more than six million Jews and others who lost their lives, because pastors and other Christians were neither "light" nor "salt" in the political process on their watch. Christians of that era did not understand the times, and they did not know what to do. Pastor Miller helps us to understand our times, so wise action can be taken by American Christians today.

Niemöller repented. He had a change of mind where one thinks—that resulted in a change of heart where one decides—concluding with a change of behavior in one's corporal life. He confessed his responsibility and accepted his guilt publicly as he spoke about his own complicity in Nazism. Niemöller's powerful words about guilt and responsibility still clutch at our consciences and hearts today. My dear fellow pastor, you and I do not have to make the same mistake that our dear brother Niemöller made.

Like the mighty men of old, you and I can understand our times so that we will know what to do. Pastor Ray Miller lifts us up in that task.

That visionary pastor (and US president) James A. Garfield warned us:

> Now more than ever the people are responsible for the character of their Congress. If that body be ignorant, reckless, and corrupt, it is because the people tolerate ignorance, recklessness, and corruption. If it be intelligent, brave, and pure, it is because the people demand these high qualities to represent them in the national legislature . . . If the next centennial does not find us a great nation . . . it will be because those who represent the enterprise, the culture, and the morality of the nation do not aid in controlling the political forces.[2]

By day, Garfield fought the Civil War to free slaves while serving in the US House of Representatives (nine terms). By night, he preached the gospel of Jesus Christ and baptized repentant sinners in nearby Washington, DC, churches. His life and his diary show no compartmentalization between the sacred and secular, faith and reason, church and state, politics and religion. These heresies impregnated themselves in the minds and lives of American Christians in decades that followed. Garfield spoke openly of both politics and religion in public—constantly—long before philosophers, Supreme Court judges, the political left, politicians such as Senator Lyndon B. Johnson in his 501(c)3 status for churches, public school teachers, university professors, and evangelical preachers taught Christians to be silent about what God has to say about the affairs of men in government and politics.

Garfield serves as a role model for pastors of all generations in proclaiming by word and deed that Jesus is Lord of all reality and has something to say about all reality, not just including the political realm but especially in the political realm. Pastor Ray Miller in *Reclaiming the Political Process* shines light on a way forward for today's pastors and ordinary Christians as Pastor/President James

2. "James A. Garfield."

A. Garfield did in his lifetime. This pastor/president warned that America will cease to be great—morally and materially—". . . because those who represent the enterprise, the culture, and the morality of the nation do not aid in controlling the political forces." American Christians for four generations now have failed in that duty. It's past time to get back in the fight.

That prophetic pastor Francis A. Schaeffer warned us in *Whatever Happened to the Human Race?*:

> That there is any respite from evil is due to some courageous people who, on the basis of personal philosophies, had led campaigns against the ill-treatment and misuse of individuals . . . we feel strongly that we stand today on the edge of a great abyss.[3]

Schaeffer keenly understood that Christians, including pastors, for the sake of their personal peace and affluence would remain silent in the face of evil itself as the church and American society today stands on the edge of that great abyss. The great abyss becomes more vivid as the carnage of slaughtered unborn children mounts and governments destroy the God-given bond between parent and child as they seize born children regardless of age and mark them for physical mutilation in the name of that empty and deceptive idolatry, transgenderism. In a spirit of covenantal invitation that God displayed at the foot of Sinai, Pastor Ray Miller beckons Christians today to abandon our personal peace and affluence and get back into the battle into which we were born for such a time as this.

A private word to pastors. The shepherd's crook has two ends. There's the end with the curve used to rescue those little lambs on the precipice of danger. Then there's the blunt end used to beat the daylights out of the lion and the bear who threaten the flock. Israel's shepherd lad David gave us this example. And now you, pastor, hold that shepherd's crook. Will you use your crook to rescue and defend God's flock of which he has made you a shepherd, or

---

3. Koop and Schaeffer, *Whatever Happened*, 1.

will you quietly leave it in the closet except to display it for special ceremonial events? The choice is yours.

A word to all Christians reading these words. Will we "Little Christs"—"Christians"—have the courage and boldness of the Hebrew women who hold the honor to be the first ever recorded heroines in holy writ to stand in rebellion against the totalitarian Egyptian government to say, "No! You cannot have our sons!"?

As Henry Blackaby said, "If things are getting darker, the problem is with us."[4] Bad theology brought us to where we are today. The problem is internal to the church, and the remedy is also within the church. What will it take for Christians, especially pastors, to wake up? Ray Miller, with this book, has made a significant contribution toward that much needed wake-up call for common everyday Christians to understand the times so they know what they can do, *and take action.*

Without taking on partisan tones, Pastor Miller steps into this breach with help for pastors and ordinary Christians. This book has real life, down-to-earth answers.

Pastor, just like teens with questions about sex will get answers somewhere, if your flock doesn't get answers from you about what their relationship to government and politics is to be, they will get them from someone. The answers they get may not be biblical. If a seriously committed Christian cannot go to his or her pastor to get clear Bible answers to the honest question, "What does God expect my relationship to the state to look like?" where can they go?

During my four years at Focus on the Family's public policy department, CitizenLink, I saw, firsthand, dedicated Christian men and women lose political races at the local, state, and national levels only because "faithful" Christians did not show up to vote. Much of the hostile-to-Christian activity we see today could have been averted if Christians in previous decades had spoken up. Many Christians have never heard that they are the stewards of their vote and will be held accountable to God for burying it.

---

4. "If Things Are Getting Darker."

Just as this foreword to this book may have encouraged you to read its contents, my prayer is that Pastor Ray Miller's book will be a foreword to an enduring Christian renewal movement where Jesus is seen as Lord over all domains of Christian living.

CONGRESSMAN BILL REDMOND, RETIRED
Masters of Divinity, Lincoln Christian Seminary
Author of *How to Run for Office as a Christian Conservative*
Los Alamos, NM
In the Year of our Lord, November 2023

Preface

THE WORD "THEOLOGY" CAN raise all kinds of emotions and reactions in Christians. If you have ever taken a theology class of some kind, you may have come away thinking, "This was the biggest waste of time I've had in a while." And if you had to pay for the class, you felt the pain even more.

It's also possible that you have taken a different theology class and come away with a completely different feeling about it. Instead of this class being a good antidote for insomnia, you actually got something out of it. Maybe you were even challenged to grow in your relationship with God and your involvement in his work through what you studied.

What's the difference? Maybe it was the instructor. I sincerely hope you had a good one who was passionate about the subject and about helping students to understand and appreciate it. But even the best instructor will be challenged by the prospect of teaching twenty-first century students to understand Calvinism's TULIP summary of what Christians are to believe about salvation. Or how to explain the Arminian position on free will. Why do these topics seem so blasé and irrelevant to today's Christians? It's not necessarily that they are unimportant. It's that most American Christians are not wrestling with the issues behind these ideas or kinds of questions.

You see, theology is not (or at least should not be) primarily the topic of the lecture hall or classroom. Real theology will, or at least should, find its way there. But it is primarily done in the midst of the "stuff" of life—the "stuff" that the current generation of those who want God to work through them to fulfill Christ's Great Commission are facing. That's what Paul, John, Peter, and the other writers of the New Testament were doing as they wrote. They didn't have a Bible college or seminary classroom in mind. They also didn't have a traditional Sunday school classroom setting or a "discipleship seminar" (whatever that is) in mind. They were what might be called "working" theologians.

As a conscientious disciple of Jesus seeking to know how you can best honor him by serving your generation in relevant ways, you are actually a "working" theologian. Granted, not exactly on the same plane as the writers of the New Testament. But the thing you do have in common with them is that you, through the working of the Holy Spirit, seek to apply the truth of God's Word to your life in the time and circumstances in which God has placed you in this world.

That's what this little book is about . . .

Introduction

WHY DID I WRITE *Reclaiming the Political Process: An Invitation to American Christians to Get Back in the Fight*?

I spent the majority of my teenage years either apathetic about the political process or prone to getting sucked into the vortex of the leftist ideologies and worldviews that were beginning to gain traction and credibility in the culture. After coming to Christ in 1972 at the age of 18, I began a gradual process of discovering how antagonistic the American Left had become to our unique American culture in general and to the spiritual heritage we have received from Scripture, the Judeo-Christian tradition, and Christian thinking.

Now, as we continue to slog through the third decade of the twenty-first century, the seeds that were sown and cultivated in the decades leading up to this century have taken root, broken through the soil, and grown into mature plants. And the fruit has ripened. It is now rotten, foul-smelling, and poisonous. And it confronts us no matter where we turn.[1]

Obviously, I am painting the Left with a broad brush. I realize that it is not a monolithic creature. My purpose for writing this book is not to precisely define the Left as an aspect of the American culture and political process.[2] I also do not propose policies or

1. Coulter, *Demonic*, 287–88; Cahn, *Return*, 4–15.

2. For such information, see Flynn, *Conservative History*, 1–7, 132, 371–74; D'Souza, *Death of a Nation*, 14–7. Flynn, writing in 2008, sees the unifying features of the American Left throughout its long history going back to the 1820s

an agenda that reflects a biblical framework and values. There have been a number of books on that topic.[3]

I write for the simple purpose of providing a basis for disciples of Christ who see the need to live out and express their faith in practical, meaningful ways in all areas of life,[4] including in the context of the political process.

For much of recent history, conscientious American Christians who are involved in politics, especially as candidates or as activists in campaigns, have been seen as an anomaly. "Wow, did you know that (fill in the name) is a Christian and is running for office?" It is almost a default expectation that politics is a place where biblical Christians and angels alike fear to tread.

In the last half century, the extent of significant Christian involvement in the American political process appears to have been limited and in decline. About all we do is pray general prayers in our church services or prayer meetings, and we vote sometimes if it isn't too much of a bother. Maybe we also complain to others in conversation or on social media about the condition of our nation, state, or community. Sometimes we even go so far as attending a city council or school board meeting (again, if it's not too inconvenient) when there is a hot-button topic on the agenda. Anything beyond that is not really holy ground and so is to be avoided by those who don't want to be defiled (or criticized).[5]

In this book I will address some of the lies and untruths (some implicit and others explicit) that have worked to de-motivate

---

as "hostility to religion, patriotism, the family, and free enterprise" (374). D'Souza outlines the Democrat Party's evolution from a regional (Southern US) political party in the 1820s to a North-South coalition leading up to and during the Civil War, to a coastal elitist and internationalist party today, one that has fought consistently against our founders' values and that desires to establish centralized power over the American population. One other profound observation D'Souza makes is that the same economic principle that one group labors for the economic benefit of another group has been a consistent value of the Democrat party through its equally zealous support of slavery and of socialism (198–200).

3. See for example Robertson, *Jesus Politics*.

4. Brother Lawrence, *Practice*, 9.

5. Schaeffer, *Time for Anger*, 15–25.

believers from taking an active role in the political process. I will bring Scripture to bear on those beliefs and demonstrate how they result from misunderstanding Scripture. I will also demonstrate how our failure to provide leadership in our culture and its political process have resulted in the many negatives that we currently see. Additionally, I will encourage believers to see involvement in the political process as a natural expression of their relationship with God, not as an aberration. I will then suggest practical and holistic ways in which we can live out our faith through this involvement and become long-term players in the political arena.

During the (supposedly) non-partisan local elections in the town where I live, I felt that, for a number of reasons, the time for noninvolvement was over for me. I volunteered to help in the campaign of a wonderful Christian man who was running for municipal judge. As we got involved in the training process for candidates and volunteers and began to meet other believers who were getting involved for the first time, it became obvious that God was leading many sincere, grassroots Christians into engaging the political process.

One of the exciting things that developed from that time was a weekly prayer meeting whose purpose and focus was specifically on the campaign and candidates who wanted prayer support. We met in different homes and church buildings in order to gain as wide a base of involvement as possible. Most weeks I was the one who brought a short devotional to prepare our hearts for our time of prayer. Many of the chapters and their subject matter are directly or indirectly the result of the process of preparing those devotionals.

I was not surprised to find out how much Scripture related to the subject of this book. But I was pleasantly surprised to be able to focus on that topic and sense God's direction to expand on it and to share it with you in this format.

May the Lord speak to your heart to bring blessing, encouragement, and fresh ideas to your mind as you read the following chapters!

1

How We Got Here
The Prayer of a Struggling Politician

INTRODUCTION

As BELIEVERS, WE OFTEN read passages like Ps 3 as encouragement when we're going through a hard time. There's certainly nothing wrong with that, but I want to dig a little deeper. If you read the heading at the beginning of the psalm ("A Psalm of David, when he fled from his son Absalom"), David apparently wrote it in the midst of a specific season in his life or in retrospect of having passed through that season. His experience of running from his son Absalom (2 Sam 15–18) was traumatic for him in many ways. It could have easily cost him his throne and his life. Even his heartfelt mourning for the loss of his son Absalom and the rebuke from his military leader Joab for not keeping things in perspective (2 Sam 18:19—19:7) indicate David had lost his edge as a leader and was not as effective as he had been in the past.

THE BACK STORY

Christians understand the background of this sad story and how David's sin of committing adultery with Bathsheba (2 Sam 11:1–5) and his plotting for the death of her husband Uriah (vv. 6–22) ultimately led to Absalom's rebellion.

Here is one aspect of this historic process in David's personal life and his public leadership over Israel that might not be so obvious: The ultimate cause of this spiritual and political crisis was David's failure to carry out the civic leadership responsibilities God had delegated to him. He was the commander-in-chief of Israel's army, and at an important moment he did not take the responsibility to lead them. At the end of his son Solomon's reign, the nation divided into two parts. Throughout the ensuing period of history, lawlessness, immorality, and idolatry characterized both nations, especially the Northern Kingdom. The Northern Kingdom also experienced a series of short-lived dynasties until its destruction by the Assyrians.

Notice how Absalom was able to begin his rebellion:

> He took advantage of David's gullibility that grew out of his sense of guilt for exiling Absalom (2 Sam 13:37–38).
> David's trusted advisor Joab conspired to take advantage of David's desire to be reconciled with Absalom (14:1–24).
> Absalom gradually gained David's confidence through deception (14:25–33).
> Absalom then usurped an undeserved position, power, and influence among the people (15:1–13).

As a result of this process, Absalom was able to undermine David's rule and force him to flee Jerusalem in disgrace, accompanied by only a handful of trusted advisors and a fraction of his military forces (2 Sam 15:14–18). It was apparently during this time that David wrote Ps 3!

This was not just a hard time for David personally. His family, kingdom, and the institutions that had up until that time been, in practical terms, the glue that held the kingdom together, were all in danger of being undermined or destroyed.

How did this situation come about? Many collateral causes may have contributed to it, but there was only one primary cause. This happened specifically because David had years earlier neglected his responsibility to provide the leadership God had called him to bring to his nation.

PSALM 3: A PREPARATION FOR BATTLE

With this background in mind, we can more clearly understand Ps 3 as David's prayer, calling on God in anticipation of an ultimate battle for survival. David first recognized and admitted how powerful his enemies were (vv. 1–2):

> Lord, how my enemies have increased!
> Many are rising up against me.
> Many are saying of my soul,
> "There is no salvation for him in God." Selah[1]

In human terms, David and his forces, along with any others who supported him, appeared to be a small minority. Many observers would feel there was no hope, especially since David had so obviously betrayed the trust God had given him. At least one man, Shimei, a relative of Saul, spoke the words many others must have been thinking: "Go away, go away, you man of bloodshed and worthless man! The Lord has brought back upon you all the bloodshed of the house of Saul, in whose place you have become king; and the Lord has handed the kingdom over to your son Absalom. And behold, you are *caught* in your own evil, for you are a man of bloodshed!" (2 Sam 16:7–8).

But fortunately, even in the midst of what appeared to be an inevitable defeat that originated in his failure, David did what he had learned to do in such times. He called on the Lord for help (Ps 3:3–6):

> But You, Lord, are a shield around me,
> My glory, and the One who lifts my head.

1. Unless otherwise noted, all biblical citations are from New American Standard Bible (NASB).

I was crying out to the Lord with my voice,
And He answered me from His holy mountain. *Selah*
I lay down and slept;
I awoke, for the Lord sustains me.
I will not be afraid of ten thousands of people
Who have set themselves against me all around.

For David, this prayer was not just a routine thing. It was purposeful, desperate, specific, and believing. It brought comfort and rest, at least as much as could be had in such circumstances. It strengthened him for the upcoming battle. He had learned by experience a vital truth through the effect of God's answers to such prayers in the past: the number of his opponents and the taunts of those who wanted him to fail are irrelevant if he will just be on the Lord's side.

David could now go into the upcoming battle with confidence (Ps 3:7–8):

Arise, Lord; save me, my God!
For You have struck all my enemies on the cheek;
You have shattered the teeth of the wicked.
Salvation belongs to the Lord;
May Your blessing be upon Your people! Selah

No matter David's personal failures and sins of the past, he knew God would always be faithful and he would always triumph. So, if he would commit himself to the Lord unconditionally, trusting God to bring about the result he wanted, he could face any challenge or threat. His fate as an individual was secondary. It was in God's hands, and that was now God's business. David's concern and motive now were that God be glorified and his sovereign plan be fulfilled. David knew by faith the Lord was already working to defeat the enemy. He knew salvation and victory already belonged to the Lord. Although David's men still had to fight, they would see the victory.

WHAT DOES THAT HAVE TO DO WITH US?

We have to be honest. As American Christians, we have for decades neglected our civic responsibility. We have done this because we have listened faithfully to those who say, "Keep God and religion out of politics. Keep that where it belongs—inside the four walls of your homes and churches."[2] We have allowed intimidation, real or imagined, to keep us from exercising moral and spiritual influence in our communities. We haven't been the light and salt in the world Jesus called us to be (Matt 5:13–16):

> *You are the salt of the earth; but if the salt has become tasteless, how can it be made salty again? It is no longer good for anything, except to be thrown out and trampled underfoot by people. You are the light of the world. A city set on a hill cannot be hidden; nor do people light a lamp and put it under a basket, but on the lampstand, and it gives light to all who are in the house. Your light must shine before people in such a way that they may see your good works, and glorify your Father who is in heaven.*

Like David, we're now seeing the results of neglecting the civic responsibility and the stewardship God has entrusted to us. We have been humiliated and mocked. We look like a quiet minority that should just accept our status.

And now, like David, we must call on God with a repentant heart and selfless abandon to his will. We have to go forward to face the battle and fight it. In general terms, here's what it will look like. We must:

- Repent for our apathy and neglect of our individual and corporate responsibility.

- Intercede for our community and nation.

- Ask God for direction and then get involved in the ways in which he directs us.

- Go into the battle confident that God will give victory, regardless of what it might look like or cost us to see the victory.

2. Schaeffer, *Time for Anger*, 59–78; Bennett, *De-Valuing*, 203–24.

If we will by God's grace do these things, we can be confident the victory—whatever it looks like—already belongs to the Lord.

FOR REFLECTION AND APPLICATION

1. How aware are you of the spiritual and biblical foundations on which the United States was established?

2. What specific events or processes in our history can you name that have caused us to go in different directions from our foundations?

3. What can you do to increase your own awareness of these things?

4. How, in practical ways, can you express your commitment to helping your community and nation return to its original foundation?

2

What's Really Happening in the Culture War?

INTRODUCTION

OUR GENERATION HAS BEEN experiencing what some have described as a "culture war."[1] But what's really happening is a battle between two ways of seeing, knowing, and understanding everything. Our culture is deciding if it will return to the godly foundation embraced by many who were involved in the historical process in which our beloved nation was founded, or if it will regress to a man-made (actually, a demonically inspired) one. Psalm 36 draws a comparison between these two foundations and provides a challenge for you and me.

THE REBELLIOUS (PS 36:1–4)

When the Holy Spirit describes humanity's fallen, sinful condition, the description is not tempered or inhibited by humankind's lack

1. See for example Lutzer, *We Will Not,* 19–20.

of perception or by a desire to soften the blow. This reality can sometimes be uncomfortable and offensive to people's sensitivities today. However, if we intend to take the Bible seriously, we have little choice but to accept this description and not to try to ignore, minimize, or trivialize it. It is what it is, as the popular phrase goes. If we desire his help in dealing realistically with the human condition, we are wise to work with it as God sees it.

It is notable that Ps 36:1b ("There is no fear of God before his eyes") is cited by the apostle Paul in Rom 3:18. In the Rom 3 passage, Paul is describing humanity's absolutely sinful and spiritually fallen condition.

The inward life of a sinful person (this can be seen as self-talk in Ps 36:1–2) forms the trajectory of their life (vv. 3–4). When the ungodly are described in verse 1 as having no "fear of God," the term for the Hebrew word is not the same as the one used in describing the reverential fear of the Lord (such as in Prov 1:7, 29). The ungodly here have no dread of the temporal results or of the eternal judgment that are to come as a result of their transgressions.

Our popular culture often encourages individuals to "listen to your heart." This is the theme of what ultimately are demonically inspired philosophies that drive much of the culture. This is true even of many Americans who claim a Christian orientation to their lives.

> *The issue is not whether God exists but whether he matters; not his reality but his relevance. It is the position of many people all the time; it is the position of believers some of the time—not as a stated creed but in practice.*[2]

Psalm 36:3–4 continue to describe fallen humankind's condition in terms of evil words, affections, and deeds. "Plans wickedness on his bed " is an image of being so absorbed in evil that it is second nature. Evil individuals are so caught up and consumed with their ungodly pursuits they cannot stop planning to do them, even when it is time for them to stop for rest.

---

2. Motyer, "Psalms," 508.

THE LORD (PS 36:5-9)

In considering what God is like, it's always helpful to think briefly about the contrasts of man-made deities with what Scripture says about God. Many good resources can be found to study how the deities of the nations surrounding Israel in Old Testament times were seen and understood.[3]

Heathen deities were generally understood in finite terms. For example, individual deities were often related to a particular ethnic group (which provides an ideal rationale for racism and ethnic bigotry). Deities were generally located in a particular area or region or type of topography. Each one had a limited sphere of interaction with and activity related to people (a god of war or a god of fertility). They were also involved in interactions with each other that reflected human social interactions (marriage, having children, hierarchal authority, and conflict within these contexts).

In contrast to these characteristics that reflect humanity's experiences, the attributes of the God who is revealed in Scripture are described in universal, infinite, and vivifying terms (Ps 36:5-6). The heavens and skies, mountains and great deeps express concepts of going beyond what humans could reach or understand. The Hebrews' God extends his mercy, faithfulness, righteousness, and judgments even to the places beyond humanity's capabilities.

He interacts with and enlivens his creation. He shows his loving-kindness and protection throughout it. He graciously makes holistic provisions for all parts of the creation, in both the physical realm and the spiritual one. He creates physical life itself and provides spiritual illumination and revelation.

We need to be honest with ourselves about what we are actually facing in our generation. It is another historical confrontation of good (God) versus evil (sin expressed in the world, the flesh, and the devil). This confrontation in all of its manifestations will intensify as our nation and the entire world approach the end of history.

3. See for example Elwell and Comfort, "Canaanite Deities and Religion," 254-55.

THE PRAYER OF THE RIGHTEOUS (PS 36:10−12)

This psalm is a prayer of "David, the servant of the Lord" based on his lifelong assimilation of the truth of God's revelation. He was certainly taught the Law as a child. In his youth he had learned it by practical and personal experience. Over time he had also learned it through his observation of life and nature, along with disciplined meditation on God's truth.

David offered to God a double request in this section of Ps 36. First, he asked God for his continued blessing on the righteous. He also expressed faith in the form of an imprecatory prayer[4] for the righteous to experience victory against their enemies.[5]

CONCLUSION

Compassion for people individually and corporately demands our involvement as Christians on multiple levels. First, God's revelation of himself and the values that Scripture advocate demand it. (See Jesus' teaching on the two great commandments in Matt 22:34–40.)

Second, in practical terms, the advancement of the Great Commission in our nation and throughout the entire world demands it. God's Holy Spirit can work through believers to make Christ known in any situation or circumstance. But the ideal is a peaceful, stable climate where the local church is able to work without hindrance.[6]

Third, we cannot be complacent in our current culture war in view of what this psalm teaches (along with the entirety of Scripture) about human nature and the human condition. We *must* be involved in the processes (political and otherwise) that

4. "What Is Imprecatory Prayer?"

5. At the same time, it is important to remember that in many ways, the Old Testament's focus on God's help against his enemies has been altered by the New Testament emphasis of praying for our enemies and for those who oppose God's redemptive plan.

6. See chapter 3 of this book, "Lies that De-Motivate."

will determine the direction our communities, culture, and nation will take.

We must be involved in prayer, yes. But not just in prayer. We must also be involved in practical ways. But not just in practical ways. To fail to be involved holistically is to fail. To become involved holistically is to be faithful stewards of God's world and our generation.

FOR REFLECTION AND APPLICATION

1. How convinced are you of the way Scripture describes humanity's actual condition without Christ?

2. What are some contemporary ways in which you have seen this condition expressed, justified, and normalized?

3. What are some specific, practical, relevant ways you would be willing to express God's love in Christ to the needs in your community that have resulted from humanity's rebellion against God?

3

Lies That De-Motivate Involvement

INTRODUCTION

MANY LIES, HALF-TRUTHS, AND distortions have kept Christians passive, disconnected, and uninvolved in the political process. When believers accept such things as true, they essentially elevate those ideas above Scripture. I want to briefly look at a few of them and demonstrate from Scripture the opposite is actually true: God does want his people to be active participants in the political process.

LIE #1: POLITICS IS DIRTY, SO IT DEFILES CHRISTIANS

The idea of defilement is an Old Testament concept.[1] Jesus addressed this issue in Mark 7:1–23 as he conversed with a group of religious leaders, the masses, and his own disciples.

---

1. Elwell and Comfort, "Cleanness and Uncleanness, Regulations Concerning," 291–92.

In pointing out the conflict between the current Jewish religious beliefs and practices and the Old Testament teaching, Jesus accused the leaders of actually confounding the purposes behind the Law. In requiring the various rites of ceremonial cleansing, the real issue of purity of heart and motive was lost for the sake of the appearance of outer cleanliness. Instead of recognizing inner cleansing was needed, they continually expressed their inner corruption and defiled condition through their words:

> After He called the crowd to Him again, He *began* saying to them, "Listen to Me, all of you, and understand: there is nothing outside the person which can defile him if it goes into him; but the things which come out of the person are what defile the person."
>
> And when He *later* entered a house, away from the crowd, His disciples asked Him about the parable. And He said to them, "Are you so lacking in understanding as well? Do you not understand that whatever goes into the person from outside cannot defile him, because it does not go into his heart, but into his stomach, and is eliminated?" (*Thereby* He declared all foods clean.) And He was saying, "That which comes out of the person, that *is what* defiles the person. For from within, out of the hearts of people, come the evil thoughts, *acts of* sexual immorality, thefts, murders, *acts of* adultery, deeds of greed, wickedness, deceit, indecent behavior, envy, slander, pride, *and* foolishness. All these evil things come from within and defile the person." (Mark 7:14–23)

The mindset or underlying beliefs Jesus was critiquing can be summarized in two sentences:

- Defilement is *ceremonial* and comes from the *outside* of a person.
- People are defiled by what they are *exposed to* and by what is *done to* them.

Although this can at first seem like a small distinction, it is profound. How we see defilement, its nature, and how it happens or can be avoided or overcome will determine a great deal about how we express our Christianity.

This view of what does and does not constitute defilement, and how to respond to defilement, is the very basis for why Jesus could incarnate (be Emmanuel, "God with us") and reach out to a lost, defiled world. Since defilement is already a reality within people, it does not come from outside them. It proceeds out from people through their words and actions.

In light of this, the Christian's responsibility isn't to physically separate from and avoid unholy things, situations, places, and people. The believer's responsibility is actually to let God purify his or her heart. This purification is not an end in itself, but a preparation and qualification for the Christian to enter the world (to incarnate) for the purpose of bringing God's redeeming and purifying work into a place and into lives that have already been defiled from within. Christians are called to be a purifying influence (imperfect as we often prove ourselves to be) within the political process.

LIE #2: ROM 13 SAYS WE ARE TO JUST OBEY THE GOVERNMENT

Romans 13:1–5 instructs believers:

> *Every person is to be subject to the governing authorities. For there is no authority except from God, and those which exist are established by God. Therefore whoever resists authority has opposed the ordinance of God; and they who have opposed will receive condemnation upon themselves. For rulers are not a cause of fear for good behavior, but for evil. Do you want to have no fear of authority? Do what is good and you will have praise from the same; for it is a servant of God to you for good. But if you do what is evil, be afraid; for it does not bear the sword for nothing; for it is a servant of God, an avenger who brings wrath on the one who practices evil. Therefore it is necessary to be in subjection, not only because of wrath, but also for the sake of conscience.*

It is true that in the context in which this passage was written, believers had no real voice in the government and were living under very heavy social, legal, and religious pressure. They needed to avoid actions that could provide a pretext for government officials to do them harm ("bear the sword" against them).[2]

It is important to note that under communist regimes, officials use this passage to persuade Christians to conform their beliefs and behaviors to the government's requirements. What makes this practice especially remarkable is that such officials use a book they don't believe to enforce compliance to a belief system, attitudes, and behaviors that violate the teachings of that very book.

A basic rule of hermeneutics (Bible interpretation) is to understand what the writer intended to communicate to the audience (readers) in the passage being studied.[3] On the basis of this understanding, today's interpreter can arrive at a reasonable application of that truth in the current time and situation. This is precisely what is required in order to faithfully live out what Rom 13:1–7 teaches.

One truth that Rom 13:1–5 emphasizes is that believers are to recognize and submit themselves to civil authority as an expression of their submission to God who established it.[4] How is that principle to be applied in the contemporary setting? The short answer is this: in the United States our civil authorities at every level are established and ultimately regulated through our federal Constitution. This and other founding documents make the citizens responsible for how members of civil government are selected and how the government is administered. Our system of government is participatory, and any adult who is not for some reason disqualified from participation through voting, running for office, working for a campaign and/or candidate has the right to

2. Hanson, *Dying Citizen*, 5–7.

3. Virkler, *Hermeneutics*, 15–46.

4. At the same time, Paul in Acts 22:22–29, after he was seized by Jewish zealots within the confines of the Jerusalem Temple and then rescued by the Roman garrison, was not hesitant to use his status as a Roman citizen to protect himself from unjust treatment, and ultimately to provide himself with a more credible voice in advancing the gospel.

participate in the process. To put this another way, the way that Christian citizens[5] in the United States express their submission to the government God has set in place is to actively be involved in the processes, events, and activities that determine how and by whom we are to be governed. Instead of passively sitting out of the process and unquestioningly living with the results of whoever is elected and whatever policies are adopted, Christians are to be an active and vocal influence on the process that determines these outcomes.

LIE #3: 1 TIM 2:1–2 SAYS WE SHOULD JUST PRAY FOR LEADERS

Sometimes the unspoken implication when believers are told we should limit our participation in the political process to prayer is that prayer is the only expression of our Christianity allowed. Too often, this kind of prayer is perfunctory, almost like an expression of what some have called civil religion whose purpose is to make sure we have covered all the religious bases. Such an understanding is far from what appears to be the meaning of this passage. I will take a look at the context of this passage to discover what its purpose is.

> *First of all, then, I urge that requests, prayers, intercession, and thanksgiving be made in behalf of all people, for kings and all who are in authority, so that we may lead a tranquil and quiet life in all godliness and dignity. This is good and acceptable in the sight of God our Savior, who wants all people to be saved and to come to the knowledge of the truth. For there is one God, and one mediator also between God and mankind, the man Christ Jesus, who gave Himself as a ransom for all, the testimony given at the proper time. (1 Tim 2:1–6)*

5. The concept of citizenship, as Americans know and take for granted, is something relatively few people throughout known history have experienced. See Hanson, *Dying Citizen*, 1–14.

In simple terms, Paul's purpose in writing to Timothy was to give him instruction and encouragement as Timothy led the congregation(s) in the city of Ephesus. These congregations needed to be healthy through good instruction and the formation of godly leaders. This kind of health would enable them to continue making disciples and growing numerically.

Leading up to chapter 2, Paul's directives for Timothy were:

- Stay on in Ephesus and continue to teach and to correct false teaching (1:3–11).

- Follow Paul's example and persevere through the enablement of the Spirit, in spite of the opposers and their opposition (1:18–20).

Following this, Paul continues his instructions to Timothy:

> Pray, and make sure the believers are praying (2:1–8)
> Make sure that female believers (and others, later in the book, 5:3–16; 6:1–2, 17–19) are behaving appropriately for the advancement of the gospel (2:9–15)
> Ensure the Ephesian congregations have qualified leaders (3:1–13)
> Be encouraged and stay on his task until Paul returns to Ephesus (3:14–16)

Now, we can ask the question about how praying for those in authority fits into this. First Timothy 2:1–6 can be outlined and understood in this way:

> What to do? Pray for all people and for all in authority (vv. 1–2)
> Why do it? So we may lead quiet, orderly lives (v. 2)
> For what purpose? God's desire is that all be saved and know the truth (vv. 3–4)
> How does this happen? Through the gospel (vv. 5–6)
> How do they hear/experience this? Through the proclamation/testimony of the gospel (v. 6)

The ideal is that the society and community in which the congregation exists and where the believers reside be peaceful and stable. This state is obviously beneficial for everyone regardless of their relationship with God and the church. It is also beneficial for the advancement of the good news, since many distractions, obstacles, and difficulties would interfere with proclaiming the gospel and making disciples. One reason God's people are to pray and work (especially in our context of participative democracy) for these kinds of conditions to prevail is it is the most advantageous setting for the church to minister to its community and to advance the Great Commission. Lawlessness, corruption, and violence distract believers and those outside Christ (see Acts 19:23–41 for one example).

That being said, the power of the gospel itself is not affected negatively or positively by the church's surroundings. The Spirit still works faithfully in times of crisis, danger, civil upheaval, and disaster. However, peace and order in society are the ideal. In order to foster this, churches that pray and worship, and whose members engage in redemptive ways with their community and society (including involvement in the political process), are vital.[6]

CONCLUSION

Probably as many lies and distortions about this topic exist as there are about most other aspects of God's Word. The three discussed in this chapter are common, but in no way do they exhaust the list of de-motivators for Christians to be actively and redemptively involved in the political process. But now that you have seen how these three false ideas can be exposed by understanding Scripture, you are hopefully better equipped to recognize and challenge other deceptions about this subject.

6. See Billheimer, *Destined for the Throne*, 61–63.

FOR REFLECTION AND APPLICATION

1. To what extent do you think these or other interpretations of Scripture have de-motivated you (or other believers you know) from involvement in the political process?

2. How would you respond to someone (Christian or not) who uses these or other biblical passages to convince you that you should not be involved in the political process?

3. In your personal devotions or Bible study, look for a passage that has or might be used to discourage you from exercising your responsibility as a Christian citizen. Put together a brief Bible study or devotional that encourages Christians to be involved.

4

God Loves to Work through Amateurs

INTRODUCTION

FOR ME PERSONALLY, AND I suspect for many people in the general public, the small group of individuals who have in recent history become known as the "expert class" have become a source of irritation. The stereotypical expert is dressed in an expensive suit or outfit. He or she has a degree (or maybe several degrees) from a prestigious, usually Ivy League university. Experts like this are polished speakers and have sophisticated tastes, manners, and mannerisms. They sound and look professional. But they are anything but experts.[1]

Contrary to how the expert class sees itself and how its members may believe that others see them, here are some examples of how many people actually see them: 1) they deserve none of the unquestioning credibility from us they expect to receive; 2) we probably wouldn't trust them to know how to change a flat tire or fix a clogged drain; 3) we wouldn't be comfortable with them

1. Hanson, *Dying Citizen*, 298–302. See also Sowell, *Vision of the Anointed*, 1–6.

babysitting our children for an evening or sitting with our ailing parent or grandparent for a few hours; 4) they might starve to death before they could figure out how to use an old school cookbook.

The least humorous characteristic of the expert class is they see themselves as necessary to everyone outside their class. They seem to really believe we cannot survive or function without them. In their minds, we may very well be nonessential, but they are absolutely essential. I want to assure you they have everything exactly 180 degrees backward. God highly values regular people and loves to advance his work in the world through them.

When we look at Scripture, we see God working through innumerable amateurs and everyday people to advance his work. Just by scanning a list of Old Testament heroes of the faith, you will discover most of them didn't really have much going for them in the way of connections or above average intelligence and abilities. Same thing in the New Testament.

Realizing this has not changed is encouraging. One of the exciting things happening as we approach the end of the first quarter of the twenty-first century is that many amateurs are becoming political activists and candidates at the local and national level. And many of them are coming from the ranks of everyday, average Christians who are concerned about what kind of community and nation they will leave to their children and grandchildren.

THE EXAMPLE OF GIDEON

In Scripture, Gideon is just one example of how God does this (Judg 6). I want to briefly review this passage to see how Gideon is a lot like today's new grassroots candidates and activists.

> Then the sons of Israel did what was evil in the sight of the Lord; and the Lord handed them over to Midian for seven years. The power of Midian prevailed against Israel. Because of Midian the sons of Israel made for themselves the dens which were in the mountains and the caves and the strongholds. For whenever Israel had sown, the Midianites would come up with the Amalekites and

the people of the east and march against them. So they would camp against them and destroy the produce of the earth as far as Gaza, and leave no sustenance in Israel, nor a sheep, ox, or donkey. For they would come up with their livestock and their tents, they would come in like locusts in number, *and both* they and their camels were innumerable; and they came into the land to ruin it. So Israel was brought very low because of Midian, and the sons of Israel cried out to the Lord.

Now it came about, when the sons of Israel cried out to the Lord on account of Midian, that the Lord sent a prophet to the sons of Israel, and he said to them, "This is what the Lord, the God of Israel says: 'It was I who brought you up from Egypt, and brought you out of the house of slavery. And I rescued you from the hands of the Egyptians, and from the hands of all your oppressors, and I drove them out from you and gave you their land, and I said to you, "I am the Lord your God; you shall not fear the gods of the Amorites in whose land you live." But you have not obeyed Me."' (Judg 6:1–10)

These verses give us a window into what formed Gideon's view of his world. He was born and grew up during a time of defeat and humiliation at the national and tribal levels. This complex of negative economic, political, military, cultural, spiritual, and social conditions was the only one he knew throughout his childhood and youth. This heartbreaking state of affairs was the result of the nation's turning away from and forgetting their covenant relationship with God.

> *Then the angel of the Lord came and sat under the oak that was in Ophrah, which belonged to Joash the Abiezrite, as his son Gideon was beating out wheat in the wine press in order to save it from the Midianites. And the angel of the Lord appeared to him and said to him, "The Lord is with you, valiant warrior." Then Gideon said to him, "O my lord, if the Lord is with us, why then has all this happened to us? And where are all His miracles which our fathers told us about, saying, 'Did the Lord not bring us up from*

Egypt?' But now the Lord has abandoned us and handed us over to Midian." And the Lord looked at him and said, "Go in this strength of yours and save Israel from the hand of Midian. Have I not sent you?" But he said to Him, "O Lord, how am I to save Israel? Behold, my family is the least in Manasseh, and I am the youngest in my father's house." Yet the Lord said to him, "I will certainly be with you, and you will defeat Midian as one man." So Gideon said to Him, "If now I have found favor in Your sight, then perform for me a sign that it is You speaking with me. Please do not depart from here until I come back to You, and bring out my offering and lay it before You." And He said, "I will remain until you return." (Judg 6:11–18)

One aspect of Gideon's situation here demonstrates that no matter how desperate the current situation is, there is power in knowing about our past. Gideon had never personally witnessed any of God's mighty miracles. He had only heard about them. How he heard about them is not certain and not really important. The fact is he knew about them because they had been passed down, probably through oral tradition in his family or tribal network. Something in those stories, in spite of what he saw as the reality around him, sparked a faith and conviction that God could still do something for them.

Another aspect of Gideon's situation reflects something of how his culture would have by default viewed him as a potential leader. He described himself to the angel as coming from the tribe and family that were lowest on the socioeconomic scale. Even if he was just self-deprecating in saying this, it reflects a belief that if God were to bring deliverance to his people, it would be better to do it through someone else (maybe an expert in delivering from the Midianites). Then, if being from the least of the least in Israel were not a sufficient disqualification, Gideon made sure the angel knew he was the youngest of his father's household. In a society that saw age and experience as possibly the greatest qualification for leadership, this certainly, in Gideon's mind, would seal the deal.

Then Gideon went in and prepared a young goat and unleavened bread *from* an ephah of flour; he put the meat in a basket and the broth in a pot, and brought *them* out to him under the oak and presented *them*. And the angel of God said to him, "Take the meat and the unleavened bread and lay *them* on this rock, and pour out the broth." And he did so. Then the angel of the Lord put out the end of the staff that was in his hand and touched the meat and the unleavened bread; and fire came up from the rock and consumed the meat and the unleavened bread. Then the angel of the Lord vanished from his sight. When Gideon perceived that he was the angel of the Lord, he said, "Oh, Lord God! For I have seen the angel of the Lord face to face!" But the Lord said to him, "Peace to you, do not be afraid; you shall not die." Then Gideon built an altar there to the Lord and named it The Lord is Peace. To this day it is still in Ophrah of the Abiezrites. Now on the same night the Lord said to him, "Take your father's bull and a second bull seven years old, and tear down the altar of Baal which belongs to your father, and cut down the Asherah that is beside it; and build an altar to the Lord your God on the top of this stronghold in an orderly way, and take a second bull and offer a burnt offering with the wood of the Asherah which you shall cut down." Then Gideon took ten men from his servants and did as the Lord had spoken to him; and because he was too afraid of his father's household and the men of the city to do it by day, he did it by night. (Judg 6:19–27)

The way Scripture describes Gideon's response to God's commission for him shows he really was not any different than we are today. He struggled with fear. More than once he struggled with it. Sound familiar?

Then Gideon said to God, "If You are going to save Israel through me, as You have spoken, behold, I am putting a fleece of wool on the threshing floor. If there is dew on the fleece only, and it is dry on all the ground, then I will know that You will save Israel through me, as You have spoken." And it was so. When he got up early the next morning and wrung out the fleece, he wrung the dew from the fleece, a bowl full of water. Then Gideon said to God, "Do not let Your anger burn against me, so that I may speak only one *more* time; please let me put *You* to the test only one *more* time with the fleece: let it now be dry only on the fleece, and let there be dew on all the ground." And God did so that night; for it was dry only on the fleece, and dew was on all the ground. (Judg 6:36–40).

We sometimes put Bible characters and heroes of the faith on a pedestal as if it only took one experience to remove all fears and inhibitions from their hearts. Not true. Gideon, like many believers today, was easily intimidated and even paralyzed by his fear of the unknown. He needed backup, encouragement, and repeated reminders and confirmation that would help him stay on task.

Gideon was not an expert. He knew it. Everyone else knew it. Most of all, God knew it. And God was happy to work with him.

CONCLUSION

Gideon's experiences show us God loves to work through amateurs to advance his work in the world (including through involvement in the political process)! That's a big reason why we desperately need each other. The Holy Spirit works through the members of the body of Christ (and not just within the four walls of the church) to provide encouragement, affirmation, and accountability.

We know the rest of Gideon's story—the rout of the Midianites and the troubles of his children. These things (both the positives in his victory and the negatives in the failures of his descendants) only highlight the reality he was not much different from us. We need to take encouragement from that. We cannot afford to see ourselves as infallible experts, the kind who can do no wrong and who live on a higher moral level than the common people that you and I really are and always have been.

Lord, please save us from the expert class and help us to always be regular people, just like Gideon!

FOR REFLECTION AND APPLICATION

1. Where do you think the assumption comes from that experts are better qualified than amateurs to lead the political process?

2. What are some de-motivating mindsets amateurs might struggle with? What are some ways to overcome these mindsets?

3. If there is an area you sense God may be directing you to be involved with, what seem to be your disqualifications? What is your answer to those? In what ways do you believe God has prepared you or is currently preparing you?

4. When God grants success, the danger of pride, presumption, and self-sufficiency exists. What can you do to guard yourself against these things?

5

Completion or Complacency?

INTRODUCTION

PLEASE READ JOSH 1:1–9; 22:1–6; 24:14–15; and Judges chapters 1–2.

In recent years, I have gotten the impression that Christians in various parts of the United States who had not previously been involved in the political process beyond voting have begun to step up and get more involved. Granted, this is hard to quantify and has been a gradual development, at some times and in some places more observable and at others less. The important thing is awareness and involvement among Christians seem to be rising. We have *entered into* the political process as an identifiable demographic. However, it now remains vital to *establish ourselves* as legitimate participants. The challenge to *persevere* in fulfilling a divine commission is one God's people have often faced. Sadly, they have not always persevered and fully met the challenge.

WE SEE THIS CYCLE IN THE BOOKS OF JOSHUA AND JUDGES

There were two broad, observable phases of God's commission to Joshua and the Israelites in the book of Joshua. The first, described in chapters 1–12, was to enter and take general control of the promised land. The second, beginning to be fulfilled in chapters 13–21, was to establish themselves as the *legitimate* stewards of the *entire* promised land, *in perpetuity*.

The book of Judges describes their failure as a nation to fully follow through and complete their God-given commission. Judges also describes the sad results of their failure. Although under Joshua's leadership they had fulfilled the first phase of their commission, they had by the end of his life only partially fulfilled the second phase. They did not fully occupy and fill the land. Thus, they failed to establish themselves as the permanent and legitimate stewards of it, ordained by God and under his covenant. They *started* well but did not *persevere* in what God had called them to do.

GOD'S REDEMPTIVE PLAN

Throughout human history, God has always been advancing his redemptive plan. Additionally, his people have always been involved as an integral part of its fulfillment. In different historical times and places, the specifics of their part have changed and varied. But regardless, God's redemptive plan and its advancement in the world have always included the participation of his people. On an individual level, a believer's life can never be complete or fulfilled without a conscious awareness of this and an intentional commitment that leads to involvement in it.

In the Old Testament and leading up to the New Testament and the coming of Jesus into the world, God's redemptive process (sometimes called salvation history) pointed initially to Abraham, his offspring, and God's promise to constitute a nation from them. God's saving purpose through and for the "seed of Abraham" in the Old Testament was to establish a holy (set apart to God and for God) people, located in a land, as a preparatory witness to the nations. Ultimately, from this people and place God's Messiah Jesus would come.

Jesus as Emmanuel ("God with us") was incarnated in that milieu. He then undertook his earthly ministry through preaching and teaching. He called and formed those who would become the leaders of the early church. He gave his life on Calvary to redeem humankind from its sins. Afterward he was raised from the dead and ascended to the Father's right hand. He gave the Great Commission to the church and promised the empowerment and direction of the Holy Spirit, which began to be fulfilled on the Day of Pentecost. Much of the remainder of the New Testament (Acts and the Epistles) tells the story of the first generation of the church. Following generations received the New Testament record as inspired by God, thus as instructive of how they were to fulfill Jesus' Great Commission throughout the world.

In the same way, we are to continue the process of making the living God known to and experienced by the world. We do this by carrying the gospel into every part of life, including the political process.

WHAT TO DO NOW

As I write this book, faithful believers in the city where I live have stepped up and taken an active role in a local election. They have achieved some notable victories in this election cycle. That is cause for celebration and the giving of thanks to God. The challenge of this time is to recognize we have only *entered into* the political process. Much remains to be done. The first step toward meeting the challenge is to recognize this is a marathon and not a sprint. It remains for us (as it did for Joshua's and succeeding generations) to *establish ourselves* as *legitimate participants* in the political process.

What is the next step? In relationship to candidates who had electoral successes and will take office, activists must provide support in specific ways. First, they and all believers must pray faithfully and specifically for them. Candidates who are entering and serving in office can set up prayer teams who are regularly given updates to enable them to pray effectively both individually and in corporate settings.

Related to prayer, believers must provide consistent encouragement and affirmation to these new office holders. These special people will be subject to the normal challenges and temptations of life and will also carry the added burdens of being targets. Their target status will be in both the spiritual realm and the more tangible realm of relationships and social pressures, being pressured to comply to values and agendas that are contrary to what originally motivated them to get involved.

Activists and other believers must also—in a responsible and informed way—hold newly elected candidates accountable to the motivations and reasons for which they first became involved in the political process. This requires sensitivity along with awareness of the political process and the particular issues each official is addressing in the office he or she holds. Everyone must also understand the limitations of what can reasonably be expected in each situation.

Finally, every believer who is actively involved in the political process must cultivate an attitude and vision for the long game. Being excited and thankful to God for momentary victories is necessary; however, staying there can lead to the same kind of complacency that defeated the ancient Israelites.

Activists must also form the habit of immediately and automatically starting to think, pray, and strategize for the next political season. This is a discipline and skill that can (and must) be learned. This predisposition for continually thinking ahead to the next campaign appears to be a mindset of many committed members of the American Left.

Human nature seems to naturally gravitate toward the familiar and comfortable. This is especially true when people are not even aware of this tendency in themselves. So be intentional and proactive about talking to other activists and possible activists about the long game.

CONCLUSION

In our Christian walk, the New Testament tells us the experiences of the Old Testament believers were intended to teach us valuable lessons about our walk with God (1 Cor 10:1–14). These lessons are about faith, obedience, trust, purity, and perseverance. They also teach us to overcome greed, idolatry, ungratefulness, and presumption.

As you read and digest this book, I trust you have begun (or are soon to begin) your involvement in the political process as a disciple of Jesus. Remember that, just as with your spiritual walk, a good beginning is necessary. But that's only the start. Each believer must also persevere and finish well. Be sure you stay with it. And bring some others with you to the finish line too.

FOR REFLECTION AND APPLICATION

1. To what extent have you observed in yourself or other believers the tendency to start well but not ultimately persevere in a lengthy or complicated task? What are some possible causes of this kind of failure? How can they be overcome?

2. Define the difference(s) between starting well and persevering. Give examples.

3. If you know a believer who has run for office and been elected, what specific actions can you take to insure they stay true to the values that motivated them to run in the first place?

6

Stand

INTRODUCTION

PLEASE READ EPH 6:10–18 and Heb 11:32–40 before continuing the chapter. These two passages provide the foundation for its content.

STAND

> Finally, be strong in the Lord and in the strength of His might. Put on the full armor of God, so that you will be able to stand firm against the schemes of the devil. For our struggle is not against flesh and blood, but against the rulers, against the powers, against the world forces of this darkness, against the spiritual *forces* of wickedness in the heavenly *places*. Therefore, take up the full armor of God, so that you will be able to resist on the evil day, and having done everything, to stand firm. Stand firm therefore, having belted your waist with truth, and having put on the breastplate of righteousness, and having strapped on your feet the preparation of the gospel of peace; in

addition to all, taking up the shield of faith with which you will be able to extinguish all the flaming arrows of the evil *one*. And take the helmet of salvation and the sword of the Spirit, which is the word of God. With every prayer and request, pray at all times in the Spirit, and with this in view, be alert with all perseverance and *every* request for all the saints. (Eph 6:10–18)

What is the repeated word or concept that keeps coming up in Eph 6:10–18? It seems to be the word "stand." Stand. Resist. Stand firm. Be alert with all perseverance.

Unconditional commitment to a noble task or responsibility that has been entrusted to someone is something our culture has traditionally held in high esteem. Americans have many pithy quotes and images that symbolize this belief: "I have not yet begun to fight," the Alamo, the Battle of the Bulge, "We shall overcome," and "Let's roll!" are some of them. One of the greatest compliments that can be given to individuals who have risked and/or given their lives for an ideal greater than self-preservation is, "He stayed at his post."

Consider this stanza to a longtime beloved song *America the Beautiful*:[1]

> O beautiful for heroes proved in liberating strife,
> Who more than self their country loved and mercy more than life.
> America, America, may God thy gold refine,
> Till all success be nobleness and every gain divine!
> (Katharine Lee Bates)

This cultural value grows out of many biblical images and messages. Here are some of them.

- David standing against the giant warrior Goliath with only a poor shepherd's weapon.
- Samson singlehandedly slaying a thousand Philistines.

---

1. "America the Beautiful."

- Daniel refusing to compromise his convictions, a decision that led to his being put in the lions' den.

- The youth Jeremiah standing, sometimes weeping, sometimes trembling, sometimes being accused of treason, before the leaders of his nation. But still standing.

- Peter in Acts 4 standing before the same court that had only recently sentenced his Lord to an agonizing death.

- And most of all, Jesus going to the cross. Because he considered obedience to the Father's will and providing for humanity's salvation to be worth more than his own life.

STAND IN FAITH

> And what more shall I say? For time will fail me if I tell of Gideon, Barak, Samson, Jephthah, of David and Samuel and the prophets, who by faith conquered kingdoms, performed *acts of* righteousness, obtained promises, shut the mouths of lions, quenched the power of fire, escaped the edge of the sword, from weakness were made strong, became mighty in war, put foreign armies to flight. Women received *back* their dead by resurrection; and others were tortured, not accepting their release, so that they might obtain a better resurrection; and others experienced mocking and flogging, and further, chains and imprisonment. They were stoned, they were sawn in two, they were tempted, they were put to death with the sword; they went about in sheepskins, in goatskins, being destitute, afflicted, tormented (*people* of whom the world was not worthy), wandering in deserts, *on* mountains, and *sheltering in* caves and holes in the ground.
> And all these, having gained approval through their faith, did not receive what was promised, because God had provided something better for us, so that apart from us they would not be made perfect. (Heb 11:32–40)

Hebrews chapter 11 is known as the Hall of Faith. In it are summarized some of the Old Testament heroes whom believers celebrate.

I have heard many sermons on this chapter over the years. In those messages I have heard some good explanations of what faith is, along with some not so good ones. The not so good ones have usually been that if we have enough faith or the right kind of faith, we can ask God for something and receive it.

The good explanations of faith usually have to do with an unconditional commitment to God and his will regardless of what that commitment may mean personally to the one exercising faith. Understanding faith in this way helps us make sense of the "and others . . ." beginning in verse 36. As I understand Heb 11, all members of the Hall of Faith had this in common (no matter what the outcome of each one's particular story was): by faith, *they stayed at their post.*

The issue that distinguishes true disciples from those who are Christian in name only is loyalty and allegiance to Jesus along with personal obedience to him and involvement in what he is doing in the world. This requires standing in faith, no matter what the outcome is for us personally.

OUR RESPONSIBILITY

Here is the bottom line for us as we respond to God's call to be active participants in the political process:

- We are not responsible for *winning the battle*; it is the Lord's battle.

- We are responsible to *stand in the battle*, no matter what the result might be.

I don't know about you, but I love the old hymns. They encourage believers to stand firm in their commitment to the Lord no matter what the cost. A couple of them are "Rise Up, O Men of

God"[2] and "Stand Up, Stand Up for Jesus."[3] These hymns remind us that, no matter what the temporal results of our struggle might be, there is more to the story. In other words, they exhort us to "stay at your post." Let's do that!

FOR REFLECTION AND APPLICATION

1. Think about a particular time when you had to take a stand alone or nearly alone. What were the circumstances? What (in spiritual, emotional, and practical terms) enabled you to do it?

2. What is your response to the idea we are responsible for our actions in a crisis but not for the ultimate outcome of the crisis?

3. What would you say or do to encourage a fellow believer who must choose whether or not to stand in a challenging situation?

2. *Rise up, O Men of God!* accessed March 8, 2024, https://hymnary.org/text/rise_up_o_men_of_god. IT should be noted that the traditional lyric was "Rise up O men of God" not "Rise up O saints of God."

3. Stand Up, Stand Up for Jesus, accessed March 8, 2024, https://hymnary.org/text/stand_up_stand_up_for_jesus_duffield.

7

Facing Your Fear

INTRODUCTION

PSALM 56 IS A *mikhtam* of David. "It is not absolutely certain what this term means, but one possibility is "record of memorable thoughts." The psalm's heading in the *Amplified Bible* says, "To the Chief Musician; set to [the tune of] 'Silent Dove Among Those Far Away.' A *Mikhtam* of David. [A record of memorable thoughts] when the Philistines seized him in Gath."[1] Psalm 56 was written to record what was happening in David's heart and mind (similar to a journal or diary) when he lived among the Philistines in Gath, hiding from Saul (1 Sam 21:10–15 and 27:1–12).

THE PROBLEM: FEAR OF MAN

> The fear of man brings a snare,
> But one who trusts in the Lord will be protected.
> (Prov 29:25)

1. *Amplified Bible* (AMP), La Habra, CA: The Lockman Foundation, 2015.

It's inevitable—God will at some point begin speaking to each of his children about the fear of mankind. I know he does this regularly with me. I believe that, with the culture of fear currently being pushed by so many authority figures in our nation and culture, this should not be surprising at all. But as a general principle for all believers in all times and places, how we respond to our natural tendency to fear people will determine the trajectory of our lives.

Here's the problem: timidity is rooted in an unbalanced concern about two things over which we have very little control. One is what people think of us or might think of us based on an action we are contemplating. The other is what might happen to us if we take a certain step or direction in life. It is not a coincidence that the word translated "timidity," "cowardice," or "fear" in 2 Tim 1:7 and "afraid" or "fearful" in Matt 8:26 are closely associated and from the same word family.[2]

> When He got into the boat, His disciples followed Him. And behold, a violent storm developed on the sea, so that the boat was being covered by the waves; but *Jesus* Himself was asleep. And they came to *Him* and woke Him, saying, "Save *us*, Lord; we are perishing!" He said to them, "Why are you afraid, you men of little faith?" Then He got up and rebuked the winds and the sea, and it became perfectly calm. The men were amazed, and said, "What kind of a man is this, that even the winds and the sea obey Him?" (Matt 8:23–27)

> For this reason I remind you to kindle afresh the gift of God which is in you through the laying on of my hands. For God has not given us a spirit of timidity, but of power and love and discipline. Therefore do not be ashamed of the testimony of our Lord or of me His prisoner, but join with *me* in suffering for the gospel according to the power of God. (2 Tim 1:6–8)

2. "1167. Deilia." I understand that making a comparison like this is not always the best way, but there are enough similarities in this case to justify this way of relating these two contexts.

Emotional manipulation and other strategies are often used in contemporary culture to facilitate this out-of-balance concern about the future or how we might be perceived by others. In order to make fear and timidity appear positive, the tactics are called things like "community sentiment" or "consensus." In the past, it has been described in negative terms like peer pressure, social pressure, and group pressure. Some of today's terms are intended to make it sound like the inducement to fear is harmless and that we should uncritically accept and submit to that inducement so we and others will be safe and accepted.

CONFRONTING OUR FEAR

This was the struggle David had, especially in the season he spent among the Philistines. Can you imagine being only a heartbeat from death practically every moment of your undercover time among your mortal enemies? All it would take is one slip, one thoughtless word or unguarded action, to bring your life to an end (Ps 56:1–11; see also Heb 13:5b–6). It's also the struggle we have.

Psalm 56:1–7 describes this emotional rollercoaster:

> Be gracious to me, God, for a man has trampled upon me;
> Fighting all day long he oppresses me.
> My enemies have trampled upon me all day long,
> For they are many who fight proudly against me.
> *When I am afraid,*
> *I will put my trust in You.*
> *In God, whose word I praise,*
> *In God I have put my trust;*
> *I shall not be afraid.*
> *What can mere mortals do to me?*
> All day long they distort my words;
> All their thoughts are against me for evil.
> They attack, they lurk,
> They watch my steps,
> As they have waited *to take* my life.
> Because of *their* wickedness, *will there be* an escape for them?
> In anger make the peoples fall down, God!

OVERCOMING OUR FEAR

The *only* real, absolute solution to fear and timidity is faith in Christ and a Spirit-disciplined thought life that overcomes timidity and defeatism. Psalm 56:8–13 give us an example of what that looks like:

> You have taken account of my miseries;
> Put my tears in Your bottle.
> *Are they* not in Your book?
> Then my enemies will turn back on the day when I call;
> This I know, that God is for me.
> *In God, whose word I praise,*
> *In the Lord, whose word I praise,*
> *In God I have put my trust, I shall not be afraid.*
> *What can mankind do to me?*
> Your vows are *binding* upon me, God;
> I will render thanksgiving offerings to You.
> For You have saved my soul from death,
> Indeed my feet from stumbling,
> So that I may walk before God
> In the light of the living.

If you are a follower of Christ and you have committed yourself to carry the gospel into every part of society, including the political process, you are part of a special fraternity. Fear is always lurking, waiting for the opportunity to hit you again. And again. This fear—the fear of people and the fear of what might happen—never entirely goes away.

But we are walking this out together. We're here to encourage one another and pray for one another. We're here to affirm and back up our candidates regardless of whether the immediate outcome looks like a victory or a defeat. And the Lord is with us every step of the way, giving us his peace. We have no reason to be carried away with fear. Instead, let's be carried away by joyous faith in the living God!

FOR REFLECTION AND APPLICATION

1. Discerning the difference between wisdom or reasonable caution and fear is not always easy. Fear can sometimes disguise itself as caution or prudence; presumption can sometimes be mistaken for faith. How can you recognize the difference?

2. How well have you done at resisting the sometimes subtle and sometimes blatant efforts of influences in our culture to normalize fear-based behavior?

3. What can you do to instill and affirm in others the kind of confidence that enables them to stand faithfully for Christ in the political arena?

8

Praying for Our Children's Education

INTRODUCTION

ONE SIGNIFICANT POLITICAL PHENOMENON of 2021 (it remains to be seen how significant it will be long term) was parents' concern with the content and conduct of primary education. It is not my purpose to discuss the specifics of what concerned parents have discovered or of what is being said or done because of their findings. Neither do I want to discuss an institutional response to their concerns.

My purpose is to briefly examine from Scripture what may motivate many of the parents who have determined to take a vocal and active stand. They seem to have either intuitively or from a conscious understanding of Scripture seen this issue as a pivotal one for their children. And they have determined to take their stand.

THREE BOTTOM-LINE QUESTIONS

I write from an unapologetically biblical view of our responsibility as American Christians to be involved in the political process. From this biblical viewpoint, I would like to explore three bottom-line questions and make some observations from four key passages that help us understand how God sees children and education.

- How does God see children?
- What does he say about children and their education?
- Where does he place responsibility for it?

GOD'S WORD

> Hear, Israel! The Lord is our God, the Lord is one! And you shall love the Lord your God with all your heart and with all your soul and with all your strength. These words, which I am commanding you today, shall be on your heart. And you shall repeat them diligently to your sons and speak of them when you sit in your house, when you walk on the road, when you lie down, and when you get up. You shall also tie them as a sign to your hand, and they shall be as frontlets on your forehead. You shall also write them on the doorposts of your house and on your gates. (Deut 6:4–9, but see vv. 1–3 also)

> Behold, children are a gift of the Lord,
> The fruit of the womb is a reward.
> Like arrows in the hand of a warrior,
> So are the children of one's youth.
> Blessed is the man whose quiver is full of them;
> They will not be ashamed
> When they speak with their enemies in the gate.
> (Ps 127:3–5)

> And they were bringing children to Him so that He would touch them; but the disciples rebuked them. But when Jesus saw *this*, He was indignant and said to them,

43

"Allow the children to come to Me; do not forbid them, for the kingdom of God belongs to such as these. Truly I say to you, whoever does not receive the kingdom of God like a child will not enter it at all." And He took them in His arms and *began* blessing them, laying His hands on them. (Mark 10:13–16)

Children, obey your parents in the Lord, for this is right. Honor your father and mother (which is the first commandment with a promise), so that it may turn out well for you, and that you may live long on the earth. Fathers, do not provoke your children to anger, but bring them up in the discipline and instruction of the Lord. (Eph 6:1–4)

HOW WE NEED TO SEE CHILDREN'S EDUCATION

Multiple sermons can be preached and lessons taught on each of these four passages. My purpose is not to do that. Rather, it is to give a quick summary of important points based on what we can learn from the above passages.

Education Is, by Its Very Nature, a Discipleship Process

Children are a gift from God and are to be seen positively by their parents as an asset in every stage of life. Education is part of the process where the value and potential that already exist are developed. Education is to be seen as a stewardship from God, to form children into something positive. Transformative teaching is to develop the student's knowledge (cognitive formation), affections and values (motivational development), and behavior (practical skills and abilities).

When children enter many educational processes such as public or secular educational institutions, they may or may not be inclined toward whatever the objectives of the process are. This is an issue especially when Christian or conservative parents send their children to schools that embrace particularly leftist, secularist agendas. When this happens, the parents discover the school and its employees may be actively undermining what they as parents have worked hard to instill in their children.[1]

Imagine stripping away all the peripheral things about education and the responsibility of all who are involved in both the formal and informal parts of a child's educational experience (parents and other family or neighborhood/community members, teachers, administrators, and curriculum writers). The essence of that child's education can be summed up in one sentence. The ideal of education is simply to prepare that child to eagerly say "yes" to the Holy Spirit when he speaks to his or her heart.

Education Should Not Be Hostile to the Bible and Christianity

Ideally, children will be taught and led to faith in Christ as part of the educational process. This should be what happens in an overtly Christian school. I have also heard from those who attended public elementary schools before the 1960s that they had prayer, Bible reading, and other daily activities that nurtured them spiritually. At the very least, the educational process for children should not be hostile or antagonistic toward the efforts that parents make to lead their children to a living faith in Christ and instill in their children the positive characteristics that will make them productive citizens.[2]

One unnecessary battle I have sometimes seen is the one between Christian parents about what is God's chosen setting for education. Homeschool parents sometimes criticize those who send their kids to a Christian school. The Christian school parents in turn criticize other Christians who send their kids to a secular private or charter school. Then they all gang up on the parents who

---

1. In some areas of the country, public education has been poisoned by curricula and personnel embedded in the educational system (at both the local level and the state level). Specific issues in curriculum are critical race theory (CRT) and gender fluidity. At the time of this writing, an exodus from public education has become necessary in such areas to save the coming generation.

2. For example, see Bennett, *De-Valuing*, 51.

send their kids to the public school. The good news is Scripture does not prescribe what the educational setting or process must look like; this is not where the fight should take place. Such bickering is a waste of time and energy. It creates mistrust and divisions in the body of Christ. The important thing is that, even if children's education (in whatever setting) is not overtly Christian, it must not work against the efforts of parents to instill positive characteristics and a genuine Christian experience in the lives of their children.

God Makes Parents Responsible for Their Children's Education

Ultimately, God will hold parents accountable for the content and results of their children's education. As the current controversies between groups of concerned parents and local school boards unfold, this mostly unspoken reality in parents' hearts drives and enlivens their grassroots movement. Parents (not the government, private school, or even the church) are ultimately responsible before God for the quality, characteristics, and outcomes of the education of children. Something that brings encouragement in such a David versus Goliath battle is that God will also strongly support, guide, and bless parents who work hard to ensure their children receive an education that honors and advances his purposes for them.

The Battle for Education Must Be Fought in the Right Place

Where is the place for concerned Christians to fight on behalf of their (and others') children? It is in the places where decisions are made about what the content, process, and desired outcomes of the children's education should be. That is because these elements of education clearly reflect the decision makers' view of what education is and should be.

Christian disciples must pray about this and then put feet to their prayers. God desires to raise up candidates and potential appointees who will be those decision makers to fill positions related to the education of children. This is true at the local level (generally elected positions) and at the state and national levels (normally by appointment).

FOR REFLECTION AND APPLICATION

1. Explain in your own words how important the education of the next generation is.

2. Interactions between parents and local school boards have sometimes become overly emotional and unproductive. What are some ways to facilitate and maintain more meaningful communication?

3. Unfortunately, many decisions about what happens at the local level are made at the state and federal levels. To what extent do local parents' concerns about their children's education reflect the importance of gaining and keeping accountability at the state and federal levels?

9

Spiritual Gifts in the Political Process

INTRODUCTION

SOMETHING TO THINK SERIOUSLY about: what if there are elements of the Left who use "dark power"[1] (violence and lawlessness; hate; demonic/occultic practices; untruth and intentional misinformation) to advance an agenda that in many respects is evil[2] and even demonic?[3] Why would Christians not desire and seek God's power through the work of the Holy Spirit to advance policies and agendas that are more in line with what he would desire and work for candidates who represent those policies and agendas? Why would we enter into a battle against evil, on behalf of what is right, while relying on our own human resources? In what other way could we more certainly guarantee the failure and defeat of our cause?

1. Ngo, *Unmasked*, 2–3; Burke, "Occult Spirituality"; Clark, "BLM Cofounder"; Hamilton Corner, "BLM Connection"; "Black Lives Matter Uses Witchcraft."

2. Abortion, the destruction of the nuclear family, the breakdown of the rule of law, and the normalization of violence as a means of advancing political agendas.

3. Coulter, *Demonic*, 287–88; Cahn, *Return,* 11–27; Washington, *Hijacked!,* 14–7.

As Christians, our involvement in the political process is part of being faithful stewards of our relationship with God. It is also an opportunity to advance the Great Commission through living out the truth of the gospel, proclaiming it, and making disciples in the process. In general terms, all we do to advance God's saving purpose in the world must be done through the power, guidance, and enablement of the Spirit. In this chapter, I want to examine how we can and must experience and manifest spiritual gifts as we are involved in the political process.

> *Now concerning spiritual gifts, brothers and sisters, I do not want you to be unaware. You know that when you were pagans, you were led astray to the mute idols, however you were led. Therefore I make known to you that no one speaking by the Spirit of God says, "Jesus is accursed"; and no one can say, "Jesus is Lord," except by the Holy Spirit. Now there are varieties of gifts, but the same Spirit. And there are varieties of ministries, and the same Lord. There are varieties of effects, but the same God who works all things in all persons. But to each one is given the manifestation of the Spirit for the common good. (1 Cor 12:1–7)*

WHAT HINDERS US?

One hindrance is the same one that often keeps believers from any meaningful involvement in the political process in the first place. We believe the world's lie that tells us to "keep your religion inside your churches and homes." Why would we need the Spirit's dynamic working outside the four walls of home and church if we believe this lie and therefore do not apply the truths of Scripture except in those limited settings?

Similarly, we often restrict the work of the Spirit through our own unbelief or self-sufficiency, all without any pressure at all from those who don't know Jesus. We isolate and try to domesticate the Spirit, limiting him to the church and home. Instead, spiritual gifts and giftedness should be at the heart of all we are and do. The work of the Spirit in the lives of believers is holistic. It encompasses every area of life:

- The home and church.
- Work and education.
- Family and extended family life.
- Neighborhood and community life (including political involvement).

A LOOK AT SPIRITUAL GIFTS

My purpose is not to present a detailed description of the gifts of the Spirit. This topic is much more broadly discussed now than it was a generation ago, thanks to the interest in and felt need among broad swaths of Christians today from many different backgrounds and traditions. I simply want to encourage believers, regardless of their church affiliation or theological understanding of the Holy Spirit, to open their hearts and minds to the reality (and the necessity) of the Spirit's work in the context of their involvement in the political process at whatever level they are involved.

Here is what I want to communicate to you: the Holy Spirit wants to work both *in* you and *through* you as you express your relationship with God through your involvement in the political process.

You can find lists of spiritual gifts in the following passages: Rom 12:6–8; 1 Cor 12:8–10, 28; 1 Pet 4:10–11. The only specific thing I will mention about what I believe about spiritual gifts is that these lists of gifts should not be understood as exhaustive, but as descriptive and illustrative.[4]

4. If the lists are seen as exhaustive, this means the gifts are limited only to those specifically mentioned. If the lists are seen as descriptive and illustrative, this means that additional manifestations of spiritual gifts may not be exactly identical. But all genuine gifts will be within the biblical parameters, such as being Christocentric, contributing to the building up of the body of Christ, and empowering and guiding the church to fulfill the Great Commission and in other ways advance God's redeeming work on the earth.

SPIRITUAL GIFTS IN THE POLITICAL PROCESS

I want to synthesize two series of things that may at first seem antithetical. To do this, I will name a specific spiritual gift[5] that is included in the New Testament lists of gifts. I will then mention activities related to the political process in which believers participate. I will then suggest ways in which that particular spiritual gift is relevant and will contribute to the process of believers' participation.

Faith: This can motivate an individual believer to have the courage and conviction to actually step out and commit to becoming a candidate for office. This is true especially in the face of today's political climate that is too often characterized by hatred and even violence.

Administration: A great need in any organization, including political campaigns and events, is for those who can "pull a miracle out of their hat" and accomplish feats that are impressive and that make the difference between success and victory or failure and defeat. When a candidate is elected to office, individuals who work behind the scenes to make things work are also invaluable.

Hospitality: Because many campaigns at the state and federal level seem to feature large events in public places, it's easy to forget about smaller events like local meetings and neighborhood forums. The ability to demonstrate winsome and competent hospitality can help to win the hearts and minds of people who are undecided.

Discerning of spirits: Regardless of how individuals may understand this gift, it involves the ability to perceive the motivations and origins of people's words or actions. It may not always be necessary or wise to verbalize what a believer has discerned through the Spirit, but that discernment will provide insight to better respond to a person or situation.

Prophecy: This gift normally has more to do with speaking to an existing situation than with predicting something in the future.

---

5. Many excellent resources are available that provide explanations and definitions of specific gifts.

Believers can speak prophetically to individuals about situations in their lives. They can also speak with an extraordinary moral authority, addressing conditions, actions, or policies and agendas that are unjust by biblical standards.

Word of wisdom, word of knowledge: While not identical, they are often understood to be complementary. A believer can be in a conversation or situation in which there seems to be no apparent resolution. Through these gifts, the Holy Spirit will reveal both information (a word of knowledge) and responses to that situation (a word of wisdom) that bring resolution. In this process and its resolution God receives glory and honor.

Teaching: The gift of teaching is much more than the ability to impart information. There is a transformative element only the Holy Spirit can provide. Christians involved in the political process, because many aspects of it have been corrupted, continually need to receive this kind of instruction and encouragement.

Leadership: Biblical leadership involves more than just skills and knowledge. It requires a genuine heart of servanthood. Excellence in leadership, accompanied by the heart of a self-giving servant, is a gift the Holy Spirit desires to impart to those who oversee the campaigns, events, and various groups or teams who are a necessary part of the political process. When a candidate is elected to office, this quality is invaluable and must be humbly sought by the office holder.

CONCLUSION

I offer these ideas and observations simply to stimulate prayerful consideration of this subject. Evil in many forms confronts God's people in America and throughout the world. We must take a stand that is beyond our natural ability. We ignore Scripture and are naïve if we do not consider the possibility that the evil our generation faces has connections to "spiritual wickedness in high places" and that this is not a spiritual battle for the soul of our nation.[6] Because

6. I am not implying the political realm is the only place where the battle is to be fought. But it is one of the arenas where God's people must aggressively

of this reality, we must run toward the battle. And we must not run in our own strength and wisdom but with what comes only from the Spirit of God.

FOR REFLECTION AND APPLICATION

1. How comprehensive do you believe and understand that the work of the Holy Spirit should be in your day-to-day life? How well does your normal, daily experience compare with that understanding?

2. Have you ever overheard or been part of a conversation outside the normal spiritual settings where it was obvious the Spirit had enabled a believer to say or do exactly what was needed in that moment? Describe how it happened.

3. Prayerfully consider areas of your life where the Spirit has given you passion, abilities, and effectiveness. How could those potentially be expressed in your involvement in the political process?

---

reassert their right and responsibility by entering, establishing themselves, and maintaining a strong and influential presence. Other areas to be addressed include entertainment, news, education, culture, and the arts. See the Appendix in this book, "The 7 Mountain Mandate."

10

The Gift Nobody Asks For

OUR BLIND SPOT (REV 12:7–12)

As SOMEONE WHO SEEKS to understand Scripture and apply it appropriately in life, one of my pet peeves is the casual way in which believers sometimes quote verses or passages without a conscientious effort to ask themselves if they are understanding and/or applying it as it was intended. One passage that too often gets this kind of treatment is Rev 12:11: "And they overcame him because of the blood of the Lamb and because of the word of their testimony, and they did not love their life *even* when faced with death."

This verse has been used to support positive confession and other beliefs that don't stand up to the tests of hermeneutics and how life in this fallen world actually is.

Here's the reality—we have a strong tendency to understand Scripture based on our worldview and the things we have experienced in life. It's impossible to completely divorce ourselves from doing this. But a good starting point is to honestly recognize this and work hard to cultivate humility and skepticism toward our default understanding of God's Word.

One series of events in Scripture that has motivated me to think about the subject of this chapter is the experiences of Elijah facing down prophets of Baal on Mount Carmel (1 Kgs 17–18) and his consequent flight from Jezebel (1 Kgs 19). One day he was putting his life and credibility as a prophet of God on the line. As a result, a season of reformation became possible. But a very short time later, he failed miserably when Jezebel threatened his life.

On Carmel, he trusted God; shortly after, he fled in total fear. What happened? There may be a number of explanations for this. But it could also be as simple as this: He failed to remember the ability to overcome the normal, default human response to such a threat comes from God's enablement.

Elijah's stand on Mount Carmel is notable because it is 180 degrees different from what most people (including believers) would do in similar circumstances. It's not normal or natural. His flight afterward is a letdown because we expect him to respond as he did before. But we all know that, left to ourselves, that is most likely what we would do if it were us. That is the normal, natural, human response.

A LOOK AT SCRIPTURE

Let's take a brief look at a couple of aspects of Rev 12:11.[1] First, the Greek word translated "testimony" is the same word that is transliterated into our English word "martyr." This is important to understand because we automatically associate physical death with this word. But generally, the idea behind it in the New Testament is being, acting as, and speaking as a witness to something or someone.

Second, they didn't "love" (from the root *agape*, to attribute high value and worth to the thing or person loved) their "life" (from the root *psuche*, not *zoe*—not so much the physical life, but the nonmaterial qualities of a life that give meaning and significance to it). Put more understandably, they were willing to risk the

---

1. My purpose here isn't to examine the larger context of this verse and the passage where it is found.

important, substantial things in their lives (up to, but not limited to physical life itself) for the purpose of faithfully maintaining their testimony of Christ. This is why, on the human level, they ultimately won the battle. They persevered no matter what the cost might personally be to them.

The way that the battle they faced is described (Rev 12:9–10) sounds a lot like what we're facing today in the United States. An incredible intensity and level of demonic deception is taking place. Although many aspects of the leftist agenda were put forward in less visible and obvious ways in the past, the same program is being advanced brazenly and unambiguously in our time. And those individuals and organizations, including churches, who oppose it are targeted.

Like Elijah on Mount Carmel, in Rev 12 these saints' commitment was not natural. They had something people don't normally have—God's enablement (a supernatural spiritual gifting). I believe this quality, the ability to risk everything of value in life, and even life itself, for Jesus and our Christian witness, can and should be seen as a spiritual gift. I call it the gift of martyrdom.

Before you think this is heresy, consider a couple of things with me. First, in areas of the world where Christians have historically been persecuted for their faith, they tend to have a theology of suffering we don't have. That theology may be written, or more oral and intuitive. The bottom line is they see martyrdom as a spiritual gift, along with the gifts we as Western Christians recognize.

Second, and much more fundamental, there is a biblical basis for this. I will briefly look at a number of passages and how they imply a gift of martyrdom most believers in America have overlooked.

The promise of Spirit-inspired speech and wisdom given in Luke 12:11–12[2] seems to be provided specifically for instances where witnesses are brought before civil/religious authorities.

---

2. "Now when they bring you before the synagogues and the officials and the authorities, do not worry about how or what you are to speak in your defense, or what you are to say; for the Holy Spirit will teach you in that very hour what you ought to say" (Luke 12:11–12).

These authorities in biblical times, unlike in twenty-first-century America, were seen as two sides of the same institution that governed the people. Today, we tend to see these things as separated and disconnected from each other, not combined. The promise to the believers in such situations is that the words they are to speak will come from outside them. The Holy Spirit will graciously grant their words.

Acts 6:3, 5, 8–15 describe Stephen as a man full of the Holy Spirit and faith, and as a spiritually gifted man who performed signs and wonders. He also confounded those who disputed his public preaching of Christ. It's easy for us to overlook what Stephen realized—every statement he made before the Jewish Sanhedrin in 7:2–53 (instead of recanting or pleading for leniency as they wanted, he seized the opportunity to preach his final sermon to the leaders of his people) made his execution certain.

Acts 7:54–60 describes Stephen's remarkable behavior and experience as he was publicly executed for his preaching. He saw a vision of heaven. As he suffered the unimaginable pain and shame of public stoning, he graciously interceded for his killers.[3]

The phrase in 1 Cor 13:3[4] that refers to surrendering the body can be understood as referring to physical martyrdom. This well-known chapter focuses specifically on the need to manifest spiritual gifts with love rather than with the various negative motivations prevalent in the Corinthian congregation. Along with the other spiritual gifts listed and inferred throughout this section of 1 Corinthians, the believers likely would have understood martyrdom as another grace gift (but probably not very high on their list of the "most spiritual" gifts) of the Spirit.

Two other passages that should mentioned are 2 Cor 11:23–28 and Heb 11:35–38. The passage in 2 Corinthians is a description of the sufferings Paul experienced specifically as a result of his commitment to carry the gospel into new areas and to establish Christian congregations there. Although people hold various views

---

3. Achtemeier, "Stoning," 994.

4. And if I give away all my possessions *to charity*, and if I surrender my body so that I may glory, but do not have love, it does me no good (1 Cor 13:3).

about how to understand this passage, the bottom line remains the same—he embraced and responded to his sufferings in ways humans normally would not do. Why? Because of the supernatural enablement he received from the Holy Spirit.

Hebrews 11:35–38 is part of the "Hall of Faith" made up of Old Testament saints. Without them, we, as Christian believers, would not be complete. Although they demonstrated the same incredible faith and commitment to God and his redemptive plan as those described earlier in the chapter, these saints experienced incredible suffering—and often death. Again, theirs is neither a natural nor normal response. As Christians, we should understand the Holy Spirit was at work in a gracious way, enabling them to prevail as God worked in the midst of the spiritual struggles of their day.

COVID-19 CHALLENGES AND THE COMING CHALLENGES

The need to respond appropriately to the leadership provided during the COVID-19 crisis gave believers in America the opportunity to grow in our understanding and experience of martyrdom. The Lord seems to be challenging us to do so. He is also challenging us to recognize and embrace the opportunity our situation brings. Although we cannot know what may be coming in the future, the Lord does. And I believe he is preparing us for it. If we want to see all that God can do to redeem lives around us and transform our communities, cities, states, and nation, we need the gift of martyrdom.

FOR REFLECTION AND APPLICATION

1. Have you ever realized you were interpreting a passage of Scripture from your own experience and/or worldview and completely missing the meaning? Describe how you came to realize this.

2. What is your reaction—emotionally, spiritually, and mentally—to the possibility God could call you or someone you love to make life-changing sacrifices for the sake of your or their Christian testimony?

3. As you prayerfully consider the direction your community, state, and nation are going, what kinds of sacrifices or risks might Christians be called by God to face?

11

Holistic Involvement

INTRODUCTION

MANY PEOPLE SEE AND navigate life with what can be described as either/or thinking. This means that one of two ideas or things can be true and valid but that it is not possible for both to be.

In a lot of ways, either/or thinking is the best way to clearly understand issues. Scripture gives us many absolutes in the areas of doctrine and morality. But there are other areas, such as how to apply and live out those absolutes in the most effective way, that need to be viewed and expressed in the most relevant or appropriate way.[1] One of those issues is how we, as Christians, understand and live out our responsibilities related to the political process.

---

1. This is not to advocate what is known as individualized or democratized truth. Basing truth on the individual's desire or personal ideology is the reason for many of today's societal ills. As the popular saying goes, wishing something were so does not make it so.

THE ISSUE

A topic that is rarely discussed openly (and at other times is hotly debated) is precisely how Christians, as citizens of heaven, are to relate to our earthly political system. The position some believers take is an either/or one.

One view is that Christian citizens should pray and vote in elections but not be involved beyond those two expressions of their faith. This is problematic because we rarely focus prayer on the political process except on the Sunday morning before an election that will happen a couple of days hence. I could even say cynically that such prayers are fatalistic. Such an approach essentially blames God for whatever the results of the election are, because when everything is said and done, he is the one who rules over his entire creation. So, in this way of seeing things, there is really nothing we can do about it anyway except pray. The pitfall of this kind of limited involvement is God's people forfeit meaningful engagement with the process and have no real voice in governance.

The opposing view can go to the opposite extreme. Some believers dive right into politics. They get so involved and absorbed in the activities and processes they end up being nearly consumed by the experience. This universe of activity, relationships, and experiences becomes central to them. They find themselves doing everything in their own strength and in a way that may be disconnected to their Christian experience and church family. This way of approaching the political process never ends well. Loss of faith, misrepresentation of what Christianity should be, disappointments of every kind, and many other negatives can result.

HOLISTIC INVOLVEMENT

So, what is the answer? As American Christians, we have the privilege and obligation to be involved. At the same time, how we are involved will determine if we bring a blessing or a curse to ourselves and others. Will it make a positive difference in our nation, state, and community? Or will we err and potentially pay a huge price politically, relationally, and spiritually?

Holism focuses on the entirety of a concept or thing and the interrelationships between its various parts. It seeks to understand and work with the total system of the thing, rather than fragmenting it into individual parts. It also sees the whole undertaking or entity as more than just the sum of its individual parts.[2]

The concept of holism may seem at first glance to be something new or novel. The truth is holism has been with us all along. The Bible has a holistic view of humanity and human beings. We are created in God's image. There are physical, spiritual, emotional, cognitive, social, relational, and other aspects of humans, and these characteristics are vital to our humanness and our experience of being human. Each of these aspects is vital. We are altogether much more than any individual (or two or three) of these manifold parts.[3]

When we, as Christians, address life, we must also look at it in a holistic way. This includes the many aspects and compartments of our lives (education, family, work, community, and recreation), no matter how disconnected from one another they may seem. Included in all of these aspects of life is our involvement in the political process. After all, the trajectory and outcomes of the political process have a great influence on the qualities of all these other areas of life and what it will ultimately look like for us and following generations.

My main concern in this book is not to address the myriad of issues that have in our time motivated Christians to get involved in the political process. It is rather to provide those believers with a clear, concise biblical foundation for their stepping into the arena.[4] My goal in this chapter is to encourage a balanced partici-

2. This is not to imply the individual parts are unimportant or that they should not be understood individually. Holism seeks to ultimately address the whole without being inordinately occupied with any one of the parts that make up the whole.

3. Munyon, "Creation of the Universe and Humankind," 235–53.

4. My description of a biblical basis for this is very basic. A great deal more could be said to support believers' involvement. One of my hopes in writing this

pation that recognizes and reflects a holistic view of our lives as citizens of heaven who are currently residing on earth.

THE BALANCE

Believers' involvement could be described as active participation on two different levels: 1) the practical, physical, earthly, tangible realm; 2) the eternal, immaterial, spiritual realm. Each context, while clearly separate in kind and quality from the other, has an undeniable influence on the other.[5] Also, each requires our involvement in an appropriate, intentional, and sustained way. This holistic kind of involvement is not for the advancement of any particular political or policy agenda, although some policies and agendas are clearly acceptable or unacceptable to disciples of Jesus.

Practical activism can be described as nothing more complicated than showing the reality of our faith through expressing it in real-world ways (Jas 2:14–26). In this book I have explained the necessity of believers being involved in the political process. I have also described many ways in which our faith and relationship with God can be demonstrated through this.

Believing prayer[6] that is offered according to Scripture, sensitive to the working of the Holy Spirit, and obedient to God and his will, is how believers participate in the spiritual realm.

All of this is directed, empowered, and motivated through the Holy Spirit, for the purpose of glorifying God the Father and Jesus Christ the Son, and for the advancement of God's kingdom and saving work in our nation, states, and communities.

It is important to understand God directs individual believers, based on things like their passions and giftings, their natural abilities and situation in life, into specific areas of involvement. The particular area where an individual or family is involved will probably fall on one or the other side of the spectrum I have described.

book is that it will encourage many others to pray, research, and write about it.

5. Billheimer, *Destined*, 51.

6. See for example Brandt and Bicket, *Spirit Helps Us Pray*, 19–31; Billheimer, *Destined*.

It should also be understood that how and to what extent someone is involved will change throughout the various seasons of their life.

We must be gracious and not legalistic toward one another about this. As in other areas of the individual expressions of our faith in Jesus, allowing for God's sovereign calling and direction in each of his people's lives is vital. We must also trust him to direct his people individually and corporately as they seek to faithfully fulfill the stewardship he has entrusted to them.

CONCLUSION

The bottom line is: we need each other. No individual or group of individuals can do it all. This is not an either/or situation where just prayer or just activism is sufficient. It is one where the body of Christ as it was constituted can, if each part finds his or her specific place and expression of giftedness, be more than enough by God's grace to face the challenges set before it. And at the end, we can look back with joy and say, "Look what the Lord has done!"

FOR REFLECTION AND APPLICATION

1. At this point in your life, where are you on the spectrum of an appropriate balance between the areas discussed in this chapter?

2. Have you observed or experienced seasons in life where areas of involvement in ministry or community have changed, intensified, or decreased based on your age, work, family situation, or other considerations? Describe this.

3. Pray regularly that God will speak to his people and more of them will respond to his call to get involved in the political process. Look for opportunities to personally encourage others to respond and to share your story with them.

12

Practical Steps

INTRODUCTION

I HOPE THAT IN the preceding chapters I have shared information and encouragement that has made you pause for a second and say "Amen!" to yourself. I hope the feelings you have about the need to step up and do something as a believer in Jesus have been confirmed and affirmed.

But I also hope you don't just put this book down, say to yourself it was a good read, and go on to the next book. Instead, I hope you begin (or continue with) this exciting, challenging, and faith-stretching journey God has called you to travel. My prayer is God will use this book to motivate you to live out your experience with Jesus more by engaging or increasing your engagement with the political process. If that happens in your life and in the lives of other sincere disciples of Jesus you know, my purpose in writing this little book will have been fulfilled.

It remains to address the YBH (Yes, But How?) issue. Here are some seed thoughts and ideas that will hopefully be a springboard to many additional ways you and others can be involved in meaningful ways. These are just random ideas. May the Holy Spirit give you multiplied more!

GET THE KIDS INVOLVED

In a recent local campaign, I saw kids (upper elementary through high school) holding signs along the street. Guess whose signs they were holding? It wasn't for the candidate that I as a Christian would have voted for! One unspoken message that was being communicated loud and clear by posting them there was that, because there were bodies in the space of a particular candidate, there was broad support for that candidate among the electorate.

The Left seems to have few inhibitions about getting children involved in political activities, even if those activities are questionable or unethical.[1] The least Christians can do is provide opportunities for their children to participate in relevant and ethical ways in the political process, ways that are appropriate, safe, and instructive. Such experiences serve in important ways to normalize in children's minds their involvement as they grow into adulthood. These experiences will help to expose the falsehood of many of the lies that have worked to exclude sincere believers from having a voice in politics.

EDUCATE THE CHRISTIAN PUBLIC

At this time in our history, being intentional and proactive about informing and educating believers about their civic responsibilities is extremely important. For too long, congregations, spiritual leaders, and the general public have seen casting a ballot as the extent of a Christian's responsibility. We need to help others to understand this limited view is wrong. We must show them that political involvement is normal for Christians, not exceptional.

---

1. See for example, "DEPLORABLE!"

How can you do this? Just like any other endeavor, you must be committed to it based on your conviction it is a necessity. Put together information from Scripture and other sources in a way you can naturally and comfortably communicate it. Be ready to share your story about how God led you into political engagement as a disciple of Jesus.

Next, plan specific ways in which you can begin to educate others. With the permission and blessing of local church leadership, you might be able to hold a class or seminar. Maybe a life group or small group could do a study on this topic. A prayer group specifically addressing the political process (stay focused!) might be an option. Less formal fellowship times might be used to ask leading questions that will stir others' curiosity and stimulate discussion. Whatever the plan or strategy looks like, you must have one in place.

A strategy is only as good as its execution. Be committed to it and follow through with it. Prayerfully ask others who recognize the need to educate believers about this to join with you.

Finally, as objectively as possible, measure the success and effectiveness of what you have planned and executed. This process is not about your feelings or emotional security. It is about how well you are living out your part of what God has called his people to do. Critiquing effectiveness by looking at the results for the purpose of improving performance is the only way to measure how well you have done.

LINK POLITICAL INVOLVEMENT WITH MAKING DISCIPLES

An extremely important (and too often missed) part of making disciples is the failure to connect discipleship in a practical way with how people live day-to-day and the situations they face that impact their lives. You are no doubt aware of how much influence the cumulative actions and policies of local, state, and federal governments and bureaucracies have on everyday life. Discipleship, especially in the context of the American political system, can and should be expressed in practical ways.

Precious, lifelong relationships can be formed through working together on the projects that make up a political campaign. The same quality of relationships can grow out of praying together regularly for candidates, campaigns, and communities.

Additionally, engaging with the political process usually brings a person into contact with many people. The Great Commission involves relating to people on a personal basis. So, the Holy Spirit can and should be expected to facilitate many opportunities to share our faith with others.[2] The key is, just as in any other setting (work, school, and neighborhood), being sensitive and available to the Holy Spirit.

HOLD A FORUM

During my first campaign season I was looking for ways to get exposure for the candidate I was working for. I tried getting him a schedule at the 55+ gated community where I live. I also tried to get him an opportunity to speak to a local service club. Surprisingly to me (as a novice at that time), I got turned down by both entities. From that experience I realized there are other ways to get your candidate out before the people you know. If this effort looks more inclusive and involves multiple candidates, it has a much better potential to succeed.

You can ask your church to hold a candidate forum. Just be sure to schedule it with enough time to give local candidates a reasonable chance to fit it on their schedules. You can also hold (or help host) a similar kind of forum in your neighborhood or community. By doing these things, you give your candidate(s) and others running for office much-needed exposure to the electorate. You also potentially build cohesion among your neighbors and raise the potential for beginning or strengthening relationships in your neighborhood.

2. Washington, *Hijacked!*, 63–64.

Making sure such forums are done well is vital. Comfort and hospitality will make a lasting impression on attenders. The format must be well thought out ahead of time and carried out in an organized way. Questions and topics should be given to candidates well in advance. The level of audience participation should be made clear and carried out fairly. A moderator known for fairness and being unbiased is absolutely necessary in order to get maximum participation.

EXPECT THE HOLY SPIRIT TO MANIFEST HIS GIFTS

I discussed in chapter 9 how the gifts of the Spirit are such an important part of our involvement as Christians in all areas of life, including our participation in the political process. Rather than isolating these God-given gifts to spiritual compartments like church services and prayer meetings, look for ways to express them and to encourage other believers to express them through their involvement in the political process and associated activities.

Politics is one of the fronts in the battle for the soul of our beloved nation (and the world). Many of the challenges we face as Christian citizens are directly or indirectly connected to the spiritual realm. Therefore, the work of the Holy Spirit to fortify and equip us for the battle, and to work through us in the battle, is not an option we can just take or leave on a whim.

GET INVOLVED IN LOCAL GOVERNMENT

Many municipalities have opportunities for average citizens to provide input in various ways throughout the year. One of these is attending public city council, county commissioners, school board, and other meetings. Your status as a member of the community who elected these representatives reinforces your constitutional right to speak up in these meetings. Making your voice heard as a Christian citizen who speaks in an informed, disciplined, and passionate way is of extreme importance in the times in which we are living. A minority who believe in and advocate for opposing values are not at all inhibited about letting elected officials know about their view.

In many municipal governments, there may also be opportunities to serve on ad hoc committees and study groups of all kinds. These committees and groups serve to research, brainstorm, and inform elected officials and employees of local government about a multitude of concerns that are relevant to serving the community and addressing specific needs. Conscientious public servants will welcome volunteerism and input that are sincerely offered. Such experiences can especially help individual believers who are prayerfully considering a greater involvement in the local political process as candidates or activists.

HELP MAINTAIN THE INTEGRITY OF THE ELECTORAL PROCESS

An aspect of the political process that seems in many ways to have escaped the notice, or at least the attention, of many conservatives is the electoral process itself. It has been observed there is a profound difference between ballots in general and legitimate, legal votes. And this difference has been exploited to a disastrous extent.[3] As a result, potentially millions of legitimate voters have been disenfranchised and their votes essentially voided.[4]

Today's electoral process is a many layered one, offering opportunities for believers to express an incredible variety of skills and passions, including monitoring procedures at the local polling place, statistical analysis, and expertise in computer technology.

---

3. See for example Valentine, "How Wisconsin Streetfighters Disrupted."

4. On a personal note, my wife and I served for fifteen years overseas as missionaries. Every election cycle, we ordered absentee ballots and mailed them back to the United States. Since we were mailing from overseas, postage cost us $25–30 to do this each time. Fraud in the electoral process disenfranchised us and our efforts to fulfill our civic duty, in addition to the economic loss.

You can do something as traditional and practical as providing transportation for those unable to get to a polling place. A new development arising from the 2022 midterm elections is, in states where it is allowed, to set up a network for collecting (harvesting) ballots to be delivered, preferably on Election Day, to *secure, monitored* drop boxes and to polling places. All of this intimate involvement with the process is absolutely necessary to insure the voice of the people is clearly heard so it can be precisely followed.

The ballot and voting booth are, in a very real sense, sacred things. They have become that to a great extent because of the innumerable and often unimaginable sacrifices made throughout our national history. These sacrifices were made by patriots to provide and maintain the right of a free people to express their will through a fair and equitable electoral process.

CONCLUSION

Practical involvement at the local level is where the action is. With very few exceptions (maybe no exceptions), this is where political activists of all kinds have gotten their start. Believers sometimes, if they view the political process and their potential involvement from other than a local perspective, fail to get involved at all just because it all seems so overwhelming.

But, if enough of us (including you) get involved locally, in ways that are realistic and a good fit for us, we will be amazed by what we are able to accomplish. And we will inspire others to get involved. And God will be glorified.

FOR REFLECTION AND APPLICATION

1. Which one of these practical suggestions resonates the most with you? Or is there one you may have heard or thought about that was not mentioned here? Why do you like it? How can you get started?

2. If you would like to get other believers involved, do you have a plan? If so, what does the plan look like? How is it working?

13

Humility

INTRODUCTION

ONE OF THE MOST common complaints against Christians in our culture may be that we are self-righteous. While I believe self-righteousness is impossible for a true believer in Jesus Christ to have (at least on an ongoing basis),[1] slipping into ways of appearing self-righteous is easy. The only way to avoid this is to remain sensitive to the work of the Spirit in our lives as he continually works in us to conform us more and more into the image of Christ.

The Bible consistently brings us back to this. God's people, in both the Old Testament and the New Testament, are called to be separate in the core of their being from the surrounding world.[2]

1. By its nature, self-righteousness cannot be held by someone whose righteousness comes from repentance and faith in Christ. The sin of a self-righteous person includes efforts to create their own righteousness without a Savior. For Christians, rather than generating their own righteousness, it is imputed to them from outside themselves, namely Christ and his death on the cross. With a believer's righteousness coming from without, by definition he or she cannot be self-righteous.

2. This separation is clearly not relational or physical (see for example John

This separation for God and to God (holiness) is not always tangible and observable. It is always something that begins and continues to occur in our hearts at the individual and corporate levels. However this holiness is experienced, expressed, and observed, it is intimately tied to repentance.

I cannot take space to elaborate on repentance. An abundance of material is available that can help believers to understand and experience what Scripture says about it.[3] My purpose here is simply to encourage you as a believer to maintain sensitivity to the Holy Spirit as you engage the political process, and especially to respond to his voice as he points out areas where repentance is needed in your life.

PRIDE THE DESTROYER

Have you ever considered that the temptations those who succeed in the political process are often much different from the temptations faced by those who experience defeat? Experiencing defeat or disappointment is a big emotional letdown. We feel rejected and that our status and credibility have been hurt or even destroyed. The good thing about this is that, in addition to hopefully learning some valuable lessons, we are usually surrounded by people who will encourage and affirm us. In the political process, victories and defeats are usually experienced corporately.

Victory is a very different thing. Where the sting of defeat is unmistakable, the subtlety of negative emotions and impulses that can overcome us in victory is incredible. Have you ever considered how Lucifer fell from his God-given position and responsibility (see Isa 14, especially verses 11–14, and Ezek 28, especially verses 11–17[4])? A big part of the cause of his fall was pride (arrogance

---

17:13–21). A physical and relational separation from "the world" (those who do not know Christ) has unfortunately sometimes been mistakenly understood as what constitutes Christian holiness.

3. See for example, Pecota, "Saving Work of Christ," 361–62; Achtemeier, "Repentance," 861.

4. There is a great deal of discussion among scholars about how these passages are to be interpreted. However, I believe the Old Testament, including

and pomp, literally "swelling" like water that overflows and floods but that must ultimately recede). It was a haughty spirit (a high, lofty attitude toward self). These were the sins of someone who had gained a position, not lost one. But when he became proud and haughty, God removed him from that position.

Why is pride so deceptive and destructive? One reason is it is usually pretty easy to spot in others but not so easily recognized in ourselves. I can feel better about myself when I discern pride and haughtiness in someone else. Not so much if someone confronts me about getting puffed up in my accomplishments.

Another reason is pride can rear its ugly head anywhere. No one, even the most quiet and unassuming person, is immune to its subtle influence. Anyone can become proud if they fail to guard against it. This battle against pride and haughtiness in our accomplishments requires a high, consistent level of honesty and humility. There is no other way to recognize and overcome it.

RECOGNIZING THE POISON OF PRIDE

> How much better it is to get wisdom than gold!
> And to get understanding is to be chosen above silver.
> The highway of the upright is to turn away from evil;
> One who watches his way protects his life.
> Pride *goes* before destruction,
> And a haughty spirit before stumbling.
> It is better to be humble in spirit with the needy
> Than to divide the spoils with the proud. (Prov 16:16–19)

Pride, haughtiness, and an attitude of triumphalism in victory are toxic; they fight against everything that qualifies someone to provide godly and effective leadership, including in the political and governmental realm. These attitudes cannot coexist with genuine Christlike humility in a believer who is involved in the political process. To cultivate the attitude of a servant, no matter in what

---

the prophetic books, recognizes the reality of the activity of volitional beings in the spiritual/nonmaterial realm.

practical ways service might be expressed, is impossible if these toxic heart attitudes have not been acknowledged and overcome through God's grace.

By its very nature, an attitude of pride destroys our sensitivity to the guidance and work of the Holy Spirit. A proud person is arrogant and refuses to learn from others, from experiences, and from the patient rebukes of the Spirit; such a person is unteachable. As such, he or she cannot serve in any meaningful way.

In our time, Christians engaging with the political process need to be characterized by two things. First, they must have the moral authority of a prophet who can speak clearly and credibly and who can be heard by others. Second, they need the spiritual power required to face evil directly and unashamedly and to overcome it. The kind of pride and haughtiness described in Prov 16:16–19 disqualifies believers from doing that and removes the very qualities we need to provide godly and effective leadership.

OVERCOMING PRIDE

This passage, Prov 16:16–19, does not specifically mention repentance, but it describes the attitude and behavior of someone who lives a life of godly repentance. Such a lifestyle of repentance is necessary to overcome toxic pride. While this cannot be done through a formula, several underlying principles that inform believers about what it should look like can be identified.

First, a lifestyle of repentance is not just words or forms of expression. There is a spontaneity to it, growing out of a heart that is continually being transformed by the Spirit.

Second, this transformation process begins when each believer first turns to Jesus for forgiveness and receives eternal life.[5]

5. One aspect of the Left that has been observed is it offers many parallels to religion in general. One of those parallels is a "conversion" experience to those who undergo a "repentance" of sorts that is facilitated by things such as guided self-criticism. Like many counterfeits of the genuine, this self-criticism leading to ideological conversion is another substitute for actual Christian repentance and conversion through the work of the Holy Spirit. Rather than becoming humble in this newfound experience, the convert can become hostile, critical,

It becomes a perpetual, lifelong process. As believers grow, they appropriate attitudes and ways of seeing life that the Spirit establishes in them. This process requires repentance and a willingness to change; that makes life transformation possible.

Third, there is a communal way of seeing and experiencing a repentant lifestyle. Just as individual believers need to develop and grow in their own lives, this must happen corporately. We need to cultivate and model sensitivity to the transforming work of the Spirit in the church, family, parachurch ministry, and political campaign.

CONCLUSION

Sincere Christians who recognize we are in a spiritual conflict must respond to the call. We must get involved. There is no other alternative; we must engage the political process in a holistic way. It has been observed that to adopt the attitudes and strategies of our diabolical enemy is to be defeated before we even enter the spiritual battle. The tendency toward pride and haughtiness in our victories and accomplishments may well be our Achilles' heel if we fail to cultivate a lifestyle of repentance and humility before God and one another. Let's pray with King David: "Create in me a clean heart, O God; and renew a right spirit within me" (Ps 51:10, KJV).

FOR REFLECTION AND APPLICATION

1. To what extent have you considered how repentance and holiness relate to your involvement in the political process?

2. How would you respond to the idea that the temptations faced by those who win an election are different from the temptations faced by those who lose one? Why?

3. When you have success in the political process, what should you do to guard against pride? Be specific!

and judgmental toward those who have not received the same experience.

14

The Secret Ingredient

INTRODUCTION

ONE OF MY FAVORITE church fellowship activities is potlucks. There are just so many wonderful aspects to a good, old-fashioned potluck fellowship meal. Such events tend to be unhurried. They are often celebratory. It's a chance to connect with new friends or to reconnect with friends you just haven't been able to talk with (although you've had really good intentions) for ages. It doesn't cost you an arm and a leg.

And the food is (with maybe a few exceptions) to die for! Why is the food so good? I have always had fun complimenting those who enjoy cooking for others, and whose enjoyment of doing that goes on steroids when it's potluck time, by thanking them for the secret ingredient that makes their dishes so excellent and tasty. Do you know what that secret ingredient is? It's love. The love that goes into the preparation and serving makes any dish more enjoyable and memorable.

Just like the love that goes into preparing food, love should be the secret ingredient in everything we as disciples of Jesus are about, including our participation in the political process.

> If I speak with the tongues of mankind and of angels, but do not have love, I have become a noisy gong or a clanging cymbal.
> If I have *the gift of* prophecy and know all mysteries and all knowledge, and if I have all faith so as to remove mountains, but do not have love, I am nothing.
> And if I give away all my possessions *to charity*, and if I surrender my body so that I may glory, but do not have love, it does me no good.
> Love is patient, love is kind, it is not jealous; love does not brag, it is not arrogant.
> It does not act disgracefully, it does not seek its own *benefit*; it is not provoked, does not keep an account of a wrong *suffered*, it does not rejoice in unrighteousness, but rejoices with the truth; it keeps every confidence, it believes all things, hopes all things, endures all things.
> Love never fails; but if *there are gifts of* prophecy, they will be done away with; if *there are* tongues, they will cease; if *there is* knowledge, it will be done away with.
> For we know in part and prophesy in part; but when the perfect comes, the partial will be done away with.
> When I was a child, I used to speak like a child, think like a child, reason like a child; when I became a man, I did away with childish things.
> For now we see in a mirror dimly, but then face to face; now I know in part, but then I will know fully, just as I also have been fully known.
> But now faith, hope, *and* love remain, these three; but the greatest of these is love. (1 Cor 13:1–13)

SUBSTITUTE INGREDIENTS

It probably goes without saying that in our culture for the longest time, there are and have been many things that are thought to be love but are not. Unfortunately, God's people are not immune from this lack of understanding and the inevitable result of failing to love in a Christlike way. Let me share with you a few ways in which love is misunderstood.

To a great extent, we have Hollywood and our own self-centeredness to blame for this one. Love has probably been understood by everyone at one time or another as a feeling. While it is true love is at some point felt on an emotional level, the emotion itself is not love. It is emotion. It feels good. But it will decline, come back, and keep us on an ever-moving emotional rollercoaster if we let it. Love can be felt, but it is not just a feeling.

A related idea is that love is something to make me complete and whole. The problem with this idea is that love cannot be focused on self, especially just for the sake of self. It must be directed outward. Love will make a human complete but not in the way a self-focused person could ever conceive of it doing so.

A pragmatic, noble-sounding way of describing love is the saying "Love is a verb." While it is true that at some point love requires action, just about any action can be done out of motives other than love. Good actions can be motivated by fear and intimidation, selfishness, or the desire for an expected benefit.

Each of these views has an element of truth. Love can be felt. It is the necessary ingredient for a complete life. It also requires that something be done. But none of these things in itself constitutes love. Love is over and above self, feelings, and commendable actions.

THE REAL THING

It is clear from how Jesus and his ministry are described in the Gospels, and from how 1 Cor 13 describes it, that love focuses on others and their needs. This focus will at times lead to actions that express love or carry out what love requires. By focusing on others and their needs, it will sometimes bring emotions in the form of gratitude, appreciation, good will, and reciprocation. All of these positive responses should lead to positive emotions. But we do not live in a perfect world; life also teaches us good deeds are not always and automatically rewarded.

Another quality of love we see in Jesus and in 1 Cor 13 is that love seeks to work in redemptive ways.[1] It prioritizes pointing people to Jesus through our words, actions, attitudes, and treatment of others. For those who do know Jesus, it seeks to serve them by encouraging, empowering, and equipping them to grow more in their relationship with him and their transformation into his likeness.

An excellent phrase that describes the real love we as followers of Christ should have and express is "disinterested benevolence."[2] This is a term popularized by Charles G. Finney and other revivalists in the nineteenth century. Tom Stewart explains it in this way:

> *Then, disinterested benevolence may best be described as the unselfish seeking of the highest good or well-being of God and others for its own sake, because the selfless promoting of both God and man's well-being is in itself the highest good possible—which is again, disinterested benevolence . . . The loftiness of disinterested benevolence is epitomized by the self-sacrifice of the LORD Jesus Christ for the world of humanity . . . Likewise, every Christian's attempt to lay himself out for the salvation of his neighbour (sic), is also a depiction of disinterested benevolence . . . Whether the Saints are seeking the salvation or sanctification of their fellow man, it is treating every man as his neighbour, i.e., with disinterested benevolence.*[3]

The love (disinterested benevolence) that motivates believers to engage with the political process is the secret ingredient because

1. By redemptive, I mean there is something in God's saving work in Christ that will hopefully be advanced through the expression of his love in any particular situation. There are sincere Christians who believe God's love should be expressed apart from any potential or desired redemptive effect. I understand that position and agree with some aspects of it (specifically as it mirrors the idea Jesus performed some of his miracles of healing simply to display compassion). However, this view can lead to outcomes that are contrary to God's desire for all to come to Christ, if it is followed to its logical conclusion.

2. Stewart, "Significance."

3. Stewart, "Significance." Emphasis his.

it reflects and expresses God's love for humanity. It is what we see and experience in Christ and in our relationship with him. It is what we as believers are called to express and demonstrate in all of our dealings with human beings, whether they know Christ or not.

GOD'S LOVE IN POLITICS

Should the words "love" and "politics" even be uttered in the same breath? If we believe the lies that de-motivate Christian involvement in the political process, no, they should not. But if we know Jesus and understand Scripture, take it seriously, and desire to live it out in our world, the answer is a clear and unambiguous "Yes!" To separate them is to ignore God's call to express his love in a significant way in our deeply broken world.

So, make sure you get involved! Bring lots of the secret ingredient with you! And, by the grace of God, stir it in thoroughly!

FOR REFLECTION AND APPLICATION

1. In the section on substitute ingredients, which most closely describes your current understanding and experience of what love is?

2. Every believer needs to be growing more into the image of Christ. What activities, disciplines, and ways of making yourself accountable to others would help you to cultivate disinterested benevolence? In practical terms, how can you put these things into action?

Conclusion

So, when everything is said and done, what's all of this really about? The goal is renewal, the kind of renewal (some might call it revival) only God can bring—and the only kind that will glorify him alone. Only a thoroughgoing renewal, first on the personal level, and that leads to congregational renewal, has the potential to renew our land on community, regional, and national levels.

For too long the Christian community in America has treated the spiritual and political/cultural realms as two disconnected arenas. Nothing could be further from the truth. True national renewal must affect both of these aspects of life in America. Anything less is a failure to see what the living God can do. If believers enter into the political process simply to advance a political agenda, even if they win the political contest in the short term, they have already lost the ultimate battle. And the battle will in many ways be lost also if we fail to engage the political process. While true believers in Christ will still be saved and go to heaven, we will have failed to be faithful stewards of the wonderful opportunities given to us in the place in history where God in his sovereignty called us to serve him and our generation.

Just like our mandate to enter and persevere in the political process, these areas of renewal are never done. They require eternal vigilance. Success and victory can and will easily degenerate into failure. We need only look at the history of God's people in Scripture or at many other histories of the human race, including our own unique American one.

The answer is easy for the Christian to envision—honoring God in every aspect of life. But to do it with a pure and humble heart, for a lifetime, with the vision to pass it on to the coming generations, is not simple or easy. Pride, triumphalism, and addiction to power have caused the best-intentioned individuals and movements to ultimately fall.

King David understood this. Even he, in the midst of success and affluence, fell. And after confessing his sin to God, he prayed for a renewal of God's redemptive goodness in his life:

> Create in me a clean heart, God,
> And renew a steadfast spirit within me.
> Do not cast me away from Your presence,
> And do not take Your Holy Spirit from me.
> Restore to me the joy of Your salvation,
> And sustain me with a willing spirit.
> *Then* I will teach wrongdoers Your ways,
> And sinners will be converted to You.
> Save me from the guilt of bloodshed, God, the God of my salvation;
> *Then* my tongue will joyfully sing of Your righteousness.
> Lord, open my lips,
> So that my mouth may declare Your praise.
> For You do not delight in sacrifice, otherwise I would give it;
> You do not take pleasure in burnt offering.
> The sacrifices of God are a broken spirit;
> A broken and a contrite heart, God, You will not despise.
> (Ps 51:10–17)

May we always carry this prayer in our hearts.

Appendix
The 7 Mountain Mandate

I HAVE A NUMBER of concerns with the 7 Mountain Mandate approach to Christians' involvement in the political process. At the same time, I concur with one of the conclusions Michael Brown reaches in his analysis of this approach.[1] Brown emphasizes there are a wide variety of perspectives among those who believe in or are sympathetic to this view. He agrees with it to the extent that it motivates believers to be involved *as committed disciples* in these various areas of life, for the purpose of expressing their faith in the real world and as another means to fulfill the Great Commission.

However, Brown strongly disagrees with two ideas held by some advocates of the mandate. One is that all people must be converted in some sense before Christ can return. The other is that the church is mandated by Scripture to take control of these seven areas of influence in preparation for Christ's return.

I have studied a compilation of writings from leaders of the Mandate movement included in a book entitled *Invading Babylon: The 7 Mountain Mandate*.[2] Each of the citations below is taken from that book.

The mandate is tied to dominion theology: "In simple terms, dominion theology is the idea that Christian believers are called to not only preach the Gospel and win converts to Christ, but also to establish the Kingdom of God on the earth."[3] Related to this, C.

1. Brown, "7-Mountain Mandate."
2. Wallnau and Johnson, *Invading Babylon*.
3. Wallnau and Johnson, *Invading Babylon*, 10.

Peter Wagner interprets the Great Commission through the lens of dominion theology. When Jesus came to "seek and to save that which was lost," Wagner appears to interpret "that which was lost" as a reference to Adam's lost dominion over creation.[4]

A number of Scripture passages throughout the book are interpreted (I believe incorrectly) by mandate leaders in such a way as to support the mandate. I will give a few examples here. Several others can be found throughout the book.

First, citing Matt 24:14 ("This gospel of the kingdom shall be preached in the whole world as a testimony to all the nations, and then the end will come"), Lance Wallnau distinguishes the gospel of the kingdom from "this Gospel of salvation" in order to argue for Christians "invading" the seven mountains of influence in today's world.[5] While the proclamation of the gospel of the kingdom can and should include practical involvement in the "real world" in which Christians live, this engagement should be seen as an activity that serves the process of proclamation and not as something in contrast to it.

Second, Wallnau cites another passage, Luke 12:32, to assert that

> You are about to pioneer the last great chapter of the journey of the Church into the Kingdom Age. It does not matter how large the obstacles are or how slender your present resources may appear to be. Jesus is once again telling His closest followers, "Do not fear, little flock, for it is your Father's good pleasure to give you the kingdom!"[6]

This assertion seems to have nothing to do with the thrust of the passage in Luke 12, which encourages disciples to be faithful, fearless witnesses through the power of the Spirit (vv. 1–12), to be generous and to trust in God's provision to overcome greed and fear (vv. 13–33), to engage in faithful service in light of Jesus' return (vv. 34–48), and to be willing to face the relational

---

4. Wagner, "Stewarding," 102–4.

5. Wallnau and Johnson, *Invading Babylon*, 67–70.

6. Wallnau and Johnson, *Invading Babylon*, 72–73.

challenges that arise from such a commitment to the kingdom of God (vv. 49–53).

Third, Patricia King, who is involved in media and broadcasting, interprets Eph 2:1–2 ("And you were dead in your offenses and sins, in which you previously walked according to the course of this world, according to the prince of the power of the air, of the spirit that is now working in the sons of disobedience") in terms of modern aerial warfare and broadcasting on the airwaves.[7] While it is obvious demonic philosophies and messages are broadly and consistently disseminated through today's media, it could be easy to assume from such a view of this passage that the struggle is limited to the physical or cyber/digital sphere. As those engaged in a spiritual battle that has been in progress throughout history and long before the modern technologies King mentions were developed, we must not make such an unconscious assumption. With or without today's technologies, the battle for the hearts and minds of human beings that began back in the garden of Eden will continue until Jesus returns.

Related to the cases I have cited above about how Scripture is interpreted and applied is the strong emphasis by advocates of the mandate on their perceptions (usually attributed to the prophetic working of the Spirit). This topic is admittedly a challenging area of Christian experience. A wide variety of opinion among sincere believers exists about how to understand and discern the genuine work of the Spirit in the individual and corporate life of the church. I can by no means provide an answer that will satisfy everyone. My concern in this brief analysis of the mandate is that there are numerous hermeneutical/interpretation and application issues, and that there is little biblical foundation for some of the assertions and claims attributed to the Spirit's working in or speaking to or through the authors.[8]

One other vital concern should be mentioned. In practical terms, how exactly would the 7 Mountain Mandate work in nations with a cultural, political, and spiritual history and heritage

7. King, "Media Army," 144.

8. Some of these instances are found on pages 92–3, 104–05, 115–16, 147.

different from what we have inherited in the United States? A major part of American Christians' motivation in getting involved in the political process is the realization our heritage and history are so markedly unique in the world. Although there are many aspects of the mandate that American Christians can agree with and see as a call to action, how can the same kind of engagement in representative government happen in other nations, when our form of government and other cultural institutions either do not exist there or are profoundly different in nature?

I believe the most significant point the book makes is that many of the challenges we face today are a result of our failure as Christians to maintain the stewardship God has given us in the areas of influence in our culture.[9] As Christians, we can and must engage with the culture, including the political process. We must express our faith in practical ways with compassion and humility as an expression of our God-given stewardship.

9. Wallnau and Johnson, *Invading Babylon*, 63–64.

Bibliography

"1167. Deilia." Bible Hub. https://biblehub.com/greek/1167.htm.

Achtemeier, Paul J., ed. *Harper's Bible Dictionary*. San Francisco: Harper & Row, 1985.

"America the Beautiful." Library of Congress, Washington, DC, 2002. Manuscript/Mixed Material. https://www.loc.gov/item/ihas.200000001/.

Bennett, William J. *The De-Valuing of America: The Fight for Our Culture and Our Children*. New York: Simon and Schuster, 1992.

Billheimer, Paul E. *Destined for the Throne: How Spiritual Warfare Prepares the Bride of Christ for Her Eternal Destiny*. Minneapolis: Bethany House, 1975.

"Black Lives Matter Uses Witchcraft to Push Agenda." BitChute. https://www.bitchute.com/video/BPP6glmmL2qY/.

Brandt, Robert L., and Zenas J. Bicket, eds. *The Spirit Helps Us Pray: A Biblical Theology of Prayer*. Springfield, MO: Gospel Publishing House, 1993.

Brother Lawrence. *The Practice of the Presence of God*. New Kensington, PA: Whitaker House, 1982.

Brown, Michael. "Is the 7-Mountain Mandate Biblical?" The Stream, Mar 4, 2020. https://stream.org/is-the-7-mountains-mandate-biblical-or-heretical/.

Burke, Dan. "The Occult Spirituality of Black Lives Matter." Crisis Magazine, Sep 8, 2020. https://crisismagazine.com/opinion/the-occult-spirituality-of-black-lives-matter.

Cahn, Jonathan. *The Return of the Gods*. Lake Mary, FL: Frontline, 2022.

Clark, Heather. "BLM Co-Founder, LA Chapter Leader Discuss Group's Occultic Practices of 'Invoking Spirits,' African 'Ancestral Worship.'" Christian News, Aug 28, 2020. https://christiannews.net/2020/08/28/blm-co-founder-la-chapter-leader-discuss-groups-occultic-practices-of-invoking-spirits-african-ancestral-worship/.

Coulter, Ann. *Demonic: How the Liberal Mob Is Endangering America*. New York: Crown Forum, 2011.

"DEPLORABLE! San Fran Teachers FORCE Young School Children To Carry Anti-Trump Signs And Yell Hateful Chants In 'Educational Protest.'" https://en-volve.com/2019/09/22/deplorable-san-fran-teachers-force-young-school-children-to-carry-anti-trump-signs-and-yell-hateful-chants-in-educational-protest/.

D'Souza, Dinesh. *Death of a Nation: Plantation Politics and the Making of the Democratic Party.* New York: All Points, 2018.

Elwell, W. A., and P. W. Comfort. *Tyndale Bible Dictionary.* Wheaton, IL: Tyndale House, 2001.

Fitzgerald, Maggy. *A Plan for Revival: 2 Chronicles 7:14.* N.p., 2021.

Flynn, Daniel J. *A Conservative History of the American Left.* New York: Crown Forum, 2008.

The Hamilton Corner. "The BLM Connection to Witchcraft." YouTube, August 19, 2020. https://www.youtube.com/watch?v=xGJSEoirF90

Hanson, Victor Davis. *The Dying Citizen: How Progressive Elites, Tribalism, and Globalization Are Destroying the Idea of America.* New York: Basic, 2021.

"If Things Are Getting Darker, the Problem Is with Us." AZQuotes. https://www.azquotes.com/quote/821686.

"James A. Garfield - Now More Than Ever Quotes." LibQuotes. https://libquotes.com/james-a-garfield/quotes/Now-more-than-ever.

King, Patricia. "God's Media Army." In *Invading Babylon: The 7 Mountain Mandate.* Lance Wallnau and Bill Johnson, eds. Shippensburg, PA: Destiny Image, Inc., 2013, 143–56.

Koop, C. Everett, and Francis A. Schaeffer. *Whatever Happened to the Human Race?* Wheaton, IL: Crossway, 1978.

Lutzer, Edwin W. *We Will Not Be Silenced: Responding Courageously to Our Culture's Assault on Christianity.* Eugene, OR: Harvest House, 2020.

"Martin Niemöller: 'First They Came For . . .'" Holocaust Encyclopedia. https://encyclopedia.ushmm.org/content/en/article/martin-niemoeller-first-they-came-for-the-socialists.

Motyer, J. A. "The Psalms." In *New Bible Commentary: 21st Century Edition,* 4th ed., D. A. Carson, et al., eds. Downers Grove, IL: InterVarsity, 1994.

Munyon, Timothy. "The Creation of the Universe and Humankind." In *Systematic Theology, Revised Edition.* Stanley M. Horton, ed. Springfield, MO: Gospel Publishing House, 2007, 215–53.

Ngo, Andy. *Unmasked: Inside Antifa's Radical Plan to Destroy Democracy.* New York: Hatchett, 2021.

Pecota, Daniel B. "The Saving Work of Christ." In *Systematic Theology, Revised Edition.* Stanley M. Horton, ed. Springfield, MO: Gospel Publishing House, 2007, 325–74.

Robertson, Phil. *Jesus Politics: How to Win Back the Soul of America.* Nashville: Nelson, 2020.

Schaeffer, Franky. *A Time for Anger: The Myth of Neutrality.* Westchester, IL: Crossway, 1982.

Sowell, Thomas. *The Vision of the Anointed: Self-Congratulation as a Basis for Social Policy.* New York: Basic, 1995.

Stewart, Tom. "The Significance of Charles G. Finney's Disinterested Benevolence." https://www.whatsaiththescripture.com/Fellowship/Disinterested.Benevolence.html.

Valentine, Jay. "How Wisconsin Streetfighters Disrupted a Democrat Ballot-Gathering System." *American Thinker*, Nov 14, 2022. https://www.americanthinker.com/articles/2022/11/how_wisconsin_streetfighters_disrupted_a_democrat_ballotgathering_system.html.

Virkler, Henry A. *Hermeneutics: Principles and Processes of Biblical Interpretation*. Grand Rapids: Baker, 1981.

Wagner, C. Peter. "Stewarding for Reformation." In *Invading Babylon: The 7 Mountain Mandate*. Lance Wallnau and Bill Johnson, eds. Shippensburg, PA: Destiny Image Inc., 2013, 99–120.

Wallnau, Lance and Bill Johnson, eds. *Invading Babylon: The 7 Mountain Mandate*. Shippensburg, PA: Destiny Image, Inc., 2013.

Washington, Clarence, Sr. *Hijacked! How Dr. Martin Luther King's Dream Became a Nightmare, Volume 1: The Dream*. Bloomington, IN: LifeRich, 2021.

"What Is Imprecatory Prayer?" GotQuestions Ministries. https://www.gotquestions.org/imprecatory-prayer.html.